AF673207

Expressive Emojis

Adding Playful Expressions with HTML, CSS & JS

Copyright © 2024 by Stelvinsaji. All rights reserved.

This publication, "Expressive Emojis" is intended for educational and informational purposes only. No part of this book, including text and code samples, may be reproduced, distributed, or transmitted without the prior written permission of the publisher, except for brief quotations in critical reviews and certain non-commercial uses permitted by copyright law.

ISBN (Paperback): 978-93-340-5987-8

ISBN (Hardcover): 978-93-341-2655-6

For permissions, licensing inquiries, or additional copies, contact Stelvin Saji at stelvinsaji@gmail.com.

License: This work is protected under the Creative Commons Attribution-NonCommercial-NoDerivatives 4.0 International License. You are free to share the material with attribution, but commercial use and derivative works are not permitted. To view the full license, visit http://creativecommons.org/licenses/by-nc-nd/4.0/.

Expressive Emojis

Adding Playful Expressions with HTML, CSS & JS

Stelvin Saji

Author's Note

Dear Reader,

Thank you for picking up "Expressive Emojis: Adding Playful Expressions with HTML, CSS & JS". This book is crafted to make your journey through the world of web development both informative and enjoyable. My goal is to help you harness the power of HTML, CSS, and JavaScript to create vibrant, expressive emojis that bring a touch of playfulness to your projects.

As a special bonus, the book includes a comprehensive tutorial on building a "Guess the Emoji" game using NextJS, Tailwind CSS, TypeScript, and ShadCN UI. This game will not only serve as a fun project but also demonstrate how these modern technologies can work together to create a sophisticated and engaging user experience.

Thank you for joining me on this journey into the world of expressive emojis. I hope you find this book both informative and enjoyable, and that it inspires you to add your creative touches to the web. Whether you are a seasoned developer or just starting, I hope this book provides you with valuable insights and sparks your creativity. Happy coding!

Warm Regards,
Stelvin Saji - Author & Editor

Layout plan for the main animation & the game

If you're interested in checking out the layout plan for both the main animation and the game, you can easily access them through the following links. They offer a detailed look at the layout designs we've created for our animation and game.

Expressive Emojis: https://tinyurl.com/yu6vnbne

Guess the Emoji: https://tinyurl.com/mrusuw2y

Contents

Chapter 4 - Interactive Emoji Magic with JavaScript

Chapter 5 - Animating Emojis with JavaScript: Adding Life to Web Interactions

Chapter 8 - Emoji Security & Privacy Considerations

Chapter 9 - Emoji Psychology: Decoding Digital Emotions

Chapter 10 - Emojis Accross Cultures: Trends and Global Impact

Bonus Content

Emoji Riddle Challenge: Can you Decode the Symbols

From Code to Cloud: Deploying your game with Vercel

Notes

Index

Introduction

Hey there!

Welcome to a world where code and creativity collide to bring emojis to life!. In this exciting journey, we'll explore the captivating realm of Expressive Emojis, exploring how HTML, CSS, and JavaScript combine to infuse your web projects with personality and fun.

Prepare to embark on a playful adventure where emojis become more than just symbols – they become vibrant expressions of emotion and style. With the power of HTML, CSS, and JS at your fingertips, you'll learn how to animate emojis & create delightful interactions that engage and delight users.

This book promises to inspire and empower you to elevate your projects with expressive emojis. So, join me as we unleash the magic of code and bring a whole new level of playfulness to the web!

Chapter 1

Getting Started with Emojis

The World of Unicode & Emojis

In today's digital landscape, Unicode plays a pivotal role in enabling seamless communication across various platforms. At the heart of Unicode lies the universal language of emojis, those tiny icons that have become a ubiquitous form of expression in modern conversation.

The Genesis and Evolution of Unicode

Unicode was conceived in the late 1980s to address the limitations and fragmentation of existing character encoding systems. Before Unicode, different systems used various encoding schemes, leading to inconsistencies and misinterpretations of text across devices and platforms. Unicode aimed to unify these disparate systems by providing a comprehensive standard to represent text from any writing system worldwide. Unicode assigns a unique code point to each character, symbol, and punctuation mark, ensuring consistent text representation and understanding, regardless of the device or platform used. This standardization is crucial for maintaining the integrity of digital communication, enabling seamless information exchange in an increasingly interconnected world.

The Emergence of Emojis

Emojis originated in Japan in the late 1990s, created by Shigetaka Kurita, an engineer working on a mobile internet platform for NTT DoCoMo. Initially designed to facilitate more expressive communication in limited text formats, emojis quickly gained popularity for their ability to succinctly and visually convey emotions and ideas. The adoption of emojis marked a pivotal moment in digital communication, heralding a new era where visual elements became integral to text-based interactions. Recognizing their growing importance, the Unicode Consortium began incorporating emojis into the Unicode Standard, assigning each emoji a specific code point to ensure consistent representation across different platforms.

The Role of Unicode in Emoji Standardization

The integration of emojis within the Unicode framework demonstrates the flexibility and foresight of the standard. Each emoji is meticulously assigned a unique code point, akin to a digital fingerprint, ensuring its accurate interpretation and rendering across various devices and platforms. This standardized encoding system allows emojis to traverse the digital realm with fidelity to their intended meaning and appearance.

By embedding emojis into the Unicode Standard, the consortium has ensured that these expressive icons can be universally recognized and used, transcending language barriers and promoting smooth communication across diverse channels and contexts. This standardization is particularly important for maintaining the clarity and identity of emojis, preventing misunderstandings and misinterpretations from inconsistent rendering.

Emojis have transcended their origins as simple pictograms to become a powerful form of communication. They serve as a universal language, enabling users to convey emotions, reactions, and ideas with clarity and precision, often in ways that words alone cannot achieve. This visual language is especially potent in bridging cultural and linguistic gaps, fostering connections on a deeply human level. The expressive potential of emojis lies in their ability to encapsulate complex emotions and concepts in a single, easily recognizable icon. Whether it's a smiley face to express happiness, a heart to signify love, or a thumbs-up to indicate approval, emojis enhance the richness and nuance of digital conversations, making them more engaging and relatable.

The Importance of Unicode for Web Designers

For web designers, understanding Unicode and emoji encoding is crucial in navigating the evolving landscape of digital design. Mastery of these intricacies empowers designers to leverage the expressive potential of emojis, integrating them seamlessly into their designs to enhance user experience and foster meaningful connections in the digital world.

Designers must be mindful of the standardized encoding of emojis to ensure their designs are accessible and consistent across different devices and platforms. By incorporating emojis thoughtfully, designers can craft captivating user interfaces, enrich content with visual appeal, and create more immersive digital experiences that resonate with users on an emotional level.

The Impact of Unicode on Creative Expression

Unicode's role in enabling creative expression extends far beyond emojis. By providing a standardized framework for representing text and symbols from all writing systems, Unicode has laid the groundwork for a richer and more inclusive digital experience. This standardization allows for the seamless integration of diverse languages and scripts into digital content, empowering users to express themselves authentically and accurately.

Unicode has also opened new avenues for creativity, enabling designers, developers, and content creators to explore innovative ways of combining text and visual elements. From crafting multilingual websites to designing interactive applications, the possibilities for creative expression are virtually limitless, thanks to the robust and comprehensive nature of the Unicode Standard.

As we navigate the complexities of the digital age, it is vital to recognize the profound impact of Unicode on shaping how we communicate and connect. The integration of emojis into the Unicode framework is just one example of how standardization can unlock new avenues of expression and creativity, fostering a more inclusive and engaging digital landscape. By embracing the transformative potential of Unicode, we can continue to push the boundaries of digital communication, exploring new ways to connect, express, and create in an ever-evolving digital world.

Exploring the Versatility of Emojis

Emojis have transcended their original purpose as mere symbols of emotions and have evolved into powerful tools for conveying a wide range of messages and sentiments. Their versatility knows no bounds, serving as conduits for a myriad of messages and sentiments that enrich textual content with layers of meaning. Let us explore their boundless potential to engage, guide, and connect with users on a deeper level.

Emojis as Expressions of Emotion

The primary function of emojis is to convey emotions, and they do this exceptionally well. From conveying joy and laughter to articulating sadness or urgency, these expressive icons offer a rich palette for communication. A simple smiley face can brighten a conversation, while a crying face can elicit empathy. Emojis encapsulate complex emotional states in a single, recognizable image, making them invaluable for adding depth and context to textual content.

In digital communication, where tone and nuance can often be lost, emojis serve as visual cues that help convey the intended emotional undertone. For instance, a sarcastic comment paired with a winking face emoji ensures the recipient understands the playful nature of the message. This ability to bridge the gap between words and emotions creates a more immersive and engaging experience for users, fostering clearer and more meaningful interactions.

Emojis in Web Design

Beyond personal communication, emojis have become indispensable allies in the realm of web design. Acting as visual signposts, they guide users through interfaces with ease and clarity.

By strategically incorporating emojis into design elements, designers can enhance user experience by emphasizing key information, directing attention, and eliciting desired emotional responses.

1. **Enhancing Navigation**: Emojis can be used to highlight important buttons, links, or sections of a website. For example, a shopping cart icon next to a link can clearly indicate the checkout process, while a magnifying glass icon signifies a search function. These visual cues help users navigate the site more intuitively, reducing the cognitive load and improving overall usability.

2. **Emphasizing Key Information**: In addition to navigation, emojis can draw attention to crucial messages or updates. A caution symbol can alert users to important warnings or errors, while a party phopper emoji can celebrate achievements or promotions. This use of visual emphasis ensures that critical information is not overlooked, enhancing the effectiveness of communication.

Emojis as Communication Tools

The versatility of emojis extends far beyond their capacity to convey emotion; they are powerful conduits for communication in various contexts.

1. **Bridging Language Barriers**: Emojis have the unique ability to transcend linguistic barriers, making them a universal language of sorts. A thumbs-up emoji, for instance, is widely recognized as a sign of approval or agreement, regardless of the user's native language. This universality makes emojis particularly useful in global communication, where language differences can pose significant challenges.

2. **Enhancing Social Media Engagement**: On social media platforms, emojis play a crucial role in fostering engagement. Posts with emojis tend to receive higher levels of interaction, as they are more visually appealing and emotionally

resonant.

Brands can leverage this by incorporating relevant emojis into their social media strategies, creating content that is more likely to be shared, liked, and commented on.

Emojis in Brand Identity

Emojis have emerged as indispensable tools for fostering stronger connections between brands and their audiences. By integrating emojis thoughtfully and purposefully into their communication strategies, brands can forge deeper and more meaningful relationships with users.

1. **Fostering Emotional Connections:** Emojis enable brands to connect with their audience on an emotional level. By incorporating emojis that evoke joy, empathy, or excitement, brands can create content that resonates with users' feelings and experiences. This emotional connection can build loyalty and trust, fostering long-term relationships with customers.

2. **Enhancing Campaigns and Promotions:** Emojis can add a dynamic and engaging element to marketing campaigns and promotions. Whether it's a holiday-themed emoji to celebrate a special occasion or a heart emoji to promote a charitable cause, these icons can enhance the visual appeal and emotional impact of marketing efforts. This can lead to higher engagement rates and more successful campaigns.

The versatility of emojis is truly remarkable. They have evolved from simple pictograms into powerful tools for communication, design, and brand identity. With their ability to convey emotions, guide users, and transcend linguistic barriers, emojis enrich the digital landscape with moments of joy, empathy, and connection. For web designers, emojis offer a rich palette to enhance user experience and create engaging, dynamic interfaces.

For brands, emojis provide a means to establish a distinctive voice, foster emotional connections, and enhance marketing efforts.

Integrating Emojis into Web Design

Integrating emojis into web design is both an art and a science. Designers must navigate a delicate balance between visual appeal and functional coherence, ensuring that the use of emojis enhances rather than detracts from the user experience. This process requires careful consideration of audience demographics, brand identity, and contextual relevance. By approaching the integration of emojis with a discerning eye, designers can harness their expressive power to elevate user engagement and communication.

At the outset, designers must ensure that the selection and implementation of emojis align with the overarching tone and objectives of the website or application. Whether the aim is to inject a sense of playfulness into the interface, convey specific emotions, or reinforce brand messaging, each emoji must be chosen thoughtfully to resonate with the target audience.

1. **Audience Demographics:** Understanding the audience is crucial. Different demographics may respond differently to the use of emojis. For instance, a younger audience might appreciate a more liberal use of playful emojis, while a professional audience might prefer subtle, strategic emoji use. Designers need to conduct thorough audience research to tailor their emoji usage appropriately.

2. **Contextual Relevance:** Emojis should be contextually relevant to the content and the message being conveyed. Using emojis that are out of place or irrelevant can confuse users and undermine the message. Designers must ensure that emojis complement the text and add value to the communication.

Ensuring Cross-Platform Compatibility

Cross-platform compatibility and accessibility are paramount considerations in the integration of emojis into web design. Ensuring that emojis render consistently across diverse devices and environments is essential to maintaining a seamless user experience.

1. **Consistent Rendering:** Emojis can appear differently on various platforms and devices, which can affect how users perceive and interpret them. Designers need to test how emojis render on different operating systems, browsers, and devices to ensure consistency. This might involve using platform-specific emoji sets or selecting emojis that are known to render consistently across most platforms.
2. **Unicode Standardization:** By adhering to the Unicode standard for emoji encoding, designers can ensure that emojis are represented accurately and consistently. Unicode provides a comprehensive and standardized framework for emoji representation, mitigating compatibility issues and ensuring that all users can engage with the emojis seamlessly.
3. **Accessibility Considerations**: Accessibility is a critical aspect of web design. Designers should ensure that emojis are accessible to all users, including those who rely on screen readers. Providing descriptive alt text for emojis can help make them accessible to visually impaired users, enhancing the inclusivity of the design.

Practical Applications of Emojis in Web Design

Emojis can be integrated into various facets of web design, enhancing visual appeal and conveying subtle nuances of emotion and tone.

1. **User Interfaces:** In navigation menus, buttons, and icons, emojis can provide visual cues that make interfaces more in-

tuitive. For instance, using a shopping cart emoji for a checkout button or a magnifying glass emoji for a search function can enhance usability and guide users effectively.

2. **Messaging Systems:** Emojis are particularly effective in chat interfaces and messaging systems, where they can convey emotions and reactions quickly and succinctly. Integrating emoji keyboards and reaction buttons can enhance user interaction and engagement.

3. **Social Media Integration:** Social media platforms thrive on visual content, and emojis play a significant role in this context. Using emojis in social media posts can make content more engaging and relatable, encouraging higher levels of interaction.

4. **Content Presentation:** Emojis can punctuate text content, providing emphasis and breaking up large blocks of text. They can also be used in headings and subheadings to draw attention and create a visually appealing layout.

Moderation and Restraint in Emoji Usage

As with any design element, moderation is key when using emojis. Overuse or misuse of emojis can detract from the clarity and professionalism of the design.

1. **Avoiding Overuse:** While emojis can enhance user experience, excessive use can overwhelm and distract users. Designers should use emojis sparingly and purposefully, ensuring that each emoji serves a clear function and adds value to the communication.

2. **Maintaining Clarity and Professionalism:** In professional contexts, designers must strike a balance between playfulness and professionalism. Using too many emojis can make

the design appear unprofessional and cluttered. Designers should aim for a clean and coherent design that uses emojis to complement, not dominate, the content.

3. **Strategic Placement:** The placement of emojis within the design should be strategic and intentional. Designers should consider the flow of the user interface and place emojis where they naturally enhance the user experience, such as near call-to-action buttons or in areas that require emotional engagement.

The Transformative Power of Emojis

Emojis have become indispensable elements in modern web design, offering designers a versatile means of enhancing user experience and communication. From their standardized encoding in Unicode to their myriad applications in conveying emotions and messages, emojis continue to shape the digital landscape in profound ways.

1. **Enhancing User Engagement:** By adding a layer of visual and emotional appeal, emojis can significantly enhance user engagement. Users are more likely to interact with and respond to content that resonates with them on an emotional level.
2. **Creating Memorable Experiences:** Emojis can create memorable and enjoyable user experiences. A well-placed emoji can bring a smile to a user's face, making their interaction with the website more pleasant and memorable.
3. **Fostering Connection and Empathy:** Emojis can humanize digital interactions, fostering a sense of connection and empathy. In customer service interactions, for example, emojis can convey friendliness and warmth, enhancing the overall customer experience.

Integrating emojis into web design presents both challenges and opportunities. By approaching emoji integration thoughtfully and strategically, designers can enhance visual appeal, convey emotions, and create more engaging and relatable user experiences. Ensuring cross-platform compatibility and accessibility is crucial to maintaining a seamless and inclusive user experience.

Chapter 2

HTML Integration

In the digital age, emojis have become an integral part of our communication, adding nuance and emotion to our messages. However, what if emojis could do more than just sit statically on our screens? What if they could express themselves dynamically and convey a wide range of emotions?

Now, we will explore how to create expressive emojis using the power of HTML, CSS, and JavaScript.

```
<!DOCTYPE html>
<html lang="en">
  <head>
    <meta charset="UTF-8" />
    <meta name="viewport" content="width=device-width, initial-scale=1.0" />
    <link rel="stylesheet" href="index.css" />
    <script src="https://cdnjs.cloudflare.com/ajax/libs/dat-gui/0.7.7/dat.gui.min.js"></script>
    <script src="https://cdnjs.cloudflare.com/ajax/libs/simplex-noise/2.4.0/simplex-noise.js"></script>
    <title>Expressive Emojis: Adding Playful Expressions with HTML, CSS & JS</title>
  </head>
  <body>
    <canvas class="emojis"></canvas>
    <script src="index.js"></script>
  </body>
</html>
```

We begin by laying down the fundamental groundwork, sculpting a basic HTML structure that serves as the canvas upon which our emojis shall spring to life. Within this structure, we define a canvas element, a realm where our emojis will dance and play. To ensure compatibility across devices, we adorn our creation with essential meta tags, delicately encoding characters and setting viewport parameters.

In our quest for visual appeal, we go beyond simple HTML and incorporate an external stylesheet called "index.css", to lend our emojis a touch of style and grace. But style alone does not suffice, we yearn for dynamic functionality, craving the spark of life to infuse our emojis with full of energy.

However, we don't stop at just looks. We want our emojis to come to life with dynamic movements. To achieve this, we use JavaScript. We also utilize the Simplex Noise library, a sorcerer capable of summoning smooth, organic movements from the void. Through its incantations, our emojis shall sway and glide, imbued with a pulsating rhythm that stirs the soul.

But we aspire for more than just passive viewing. We want our users to feel engaged and in control. That's where the dat.gui library comes into play. This mystical artifact grants them the power to shape their experience, to sculpt the very fabric of our creation. With its interactive controls, we may tweak parameters, adjusting speeds, resizing dimensions thus crafting a personalized journey through the whimsical world of our emojis.

With HTML as our canvas, JavaScript as our brush, and the libraries as our palette, we are ready to breathe life into our expressive emojis project.

Simplex Noise Library

In the world of computer graphics and simulation, there's this awesome thing called the Simplex Noise library. It's basically magic for creating really cool, natural-looking patterns that seem totally random but actually have a sense of order to them. This library was made by Ken Perlin, who improved upon an older algorithm called Perlin Noise to make it faster and better.

Now, Simplex noise isn't just your average random noise generator. It works its magic in higher dimensions, which basically means it can create super intricate patterns with crazy precision. It does this by giving each point in space a "noise" value, kind of like adding a sprinkle of randomness to it.

But here's the cool part: instead of just slapping random values everywhere, Simplex noise makes sure neighbouring points get along nicely. It's like they're all part of the same family, resulting in patterns that look smooth and natural, rather than jarringly random.

This special property makes Simplex noise perfect for making things like terrain in video games, creating textures that look real but aren't, and even making emojis move around in a way that feels alive.

By using Simplex noise in our project, we're able to give our emojis a sense of motion and variation that makes them way more interesting than just sitting there like boring old symbols. It's like we're giving them a little spark of life, making our animations more fun and immersive for the people using them.

Here is an example animation showcasing the Simplex Noise Library:

Imagine being able to create mesmerizing, fluid animation on your web page with just a few lines of code. That's exactly what we'll be doing here by harnessing the power of Simplex Noise. This HTML setup is your gateway to a stunning visual experience that seamlessly fills your screen, perfect for backgrounds, visualizations, or just a bit of creative fun.

```html
<!DOCTYPE html>
<html lang="en">
  <head>
    <meta charset="UTF-8" />
    <meta name="viewport" content="width=device-width, initial-scale=1.0" />
    <script src="https://cdnjs.cloudflare.com/ajax/libs/simplex-noise/2.4.0/simplex-noise.min.js"></script>
    <title>Simplex Noise Animation</title>
    <style>
      body,
      html {
        margin: 0;
        padding: 0;
        height: 100%;
        overflow: hidden;
      }

      canvas {
        display: block;
        width: 100%;
        height: 100%;
      }
    </style>
  </head>
  <body>
    <canvas id="canvas"></canvas>
    <script src="index.js"></script>
  </body>
</html>
```

Here's what we're working with:

1. A full-screen canvas:

First and foremost, we'll be utilizing an HTML <canvas> element that will occupy the entire viewport of the web browser. This means that no matter the size of the screen or the device being used, our canvas will adjust to fill the entire space available. This approach ensures that our animation has the maximum impact, providing a large, uninterrupted area for our visuals to unfold.

2. Simplex Noise:

At the heart of our animation is Simplex Noise, a mathematical algorithm used to generate smooth, natural-looking patterns. Simplex Noise is a more advanced and efficient alternative to the older Perlin Noise, offering several advantages:

- **Visual Appeal:** The patterns generated by Simplex Noise are more visually appealing and less prone to the artifacts that can sometimes appear with Perlin Noise.
- **Efficiency:** Simplex Noise is computationally more efficient, meaning it can generate patterns faster and with less processing power. This is particularly important for real-time animations, where performance is key.
- **Smoothness:** The algorithm produces smooth transitions and variations, which are perfect for creating organic, flowing visuals that feel natural and engaging.

3. A clean slate:

Finally, we'll start with a clean slate, focusing on minimal styling and setup. This approach allows us to channel our efforts entirely into the creative aspects of the project.

```
// Simplex noise function
const simplex = new SimplexNoise();

// Canvas setup
const canvas = document.getElementById("canvas");
const ctx = canvas.getContext("2d");
canvas.width = window.innerWidth;
canvas.height = window.innerHeight;
```

This code serves two primary functions: generating noise and setting up a canvas for drawing within a web browser environment- First, an instance of the SimplexNoise class is created.

The next step is to select an HTML canvas element from the document. This is done using the canvas's ID attribute, which in this case is "canvas". The canvas element in HTML serves as a drawable region within the browser, allowing for the rendering of various graphics directly on the webpage.

To facilitate drawing on the canvas, the code calls the getContext("2d") method on the canvas element. This method retrieves a 2D drawing context, which is an object stored in the variable ctx. The 2D context provides a rich set of methods and properties designed for drawing and manipulating graphics on the canvas. These capabilities include drawing shapes, text, images, and other graphics operations.

To ensure the canvas occupies the entire browser window, the code sets the canvas's width and height properties to match the window's inner dimensions. Specifically, window.innerWidth and window.innerHeight return the interior width and height of the browser window in pixels. By setting the canvas's width and height to these values, the canvas is resized to fill the entire visible area of the browser window. This approach ensures that the canvas dynamically adjusts to the size of the browser window, providing a full-screen drawing area. This is particularly useful for applications like games, simulations, or any interactive graphics that benefit from utilizing the entire screen space.

```
// Wave parameters
let time = 0;
let speed = 0.02;
let waveHeight = 50;
let noiseScale = 0.02;

// Animation Loop
function animate() {
    requestAnimationFrame(animate);
    draw();
}
```

Now, we're setting up the foundation for our animation by declaring and initializing four crucial variables:

- **time:** This variable will keep track of how much time has passed within our animation. By incrementing this variable, we can control the progression of our animation over time.

- **speed:** This variable dictates how fast our animation progresses. By adjusting the speed, we can make our animation move faster or slower.

- **waveHeight:** This variable controls the height of the waves that we'll be drawing on our canvas. By modifying the waveHeight, we can create waves of varying amplitudes.

- **noiseScale:** This variable determines the scale of the noise function, which influences the smoothness and frequency of the waves we're generating. A larger noiseScale will create smoother, more gradual waves, while a smaller noiseScale will produce more frequent, choppier waves.

Once these variables are set, we move on to creating a function called animate. This function will serve as our animation loop, repeatedly updating the canvas content to create the illusion of movement.

To ensure our animation runs smoothly, we use the requestAnimationFrame(animate) method. This method schedules a call to the animate function before the browser's next repaint. By doing this, we sync our animation with the browser's refresh rate, resulting in a smooth and fluid animation experience.

Within the animate function, we will also call another function named draw. The draw function is responsible for crafting each frame of our animation. It will be called within the animation loop to dynamically update the canvas content based on the current values of time, waveHeight, and noiseScale.

As the animation loop iterates, the time variable increases by the speed value. This increment determines how quickly our animation progresses. The draw function will then use the updated time value, along with the waveHeight and noiseScale, to render the current frame of the animation.

By consistently invoking requestAnimationFrame, our animation loop creates a seamless and continuous animation effect. The browser handles the timing and synchronization, allowing us to focus on updating the canvas content and ensuring a visually appealing animation.

```
// Draw function
function draw() {
    // Clear canvas
    ctx.clearRect(0, 0, canvas.width, canvas.height);

    // Draw background
    ctx.fillStyle = "#f9f9f9";
    ctx.fillRect(0, 0, canvas.width, canvas.height);

    // Draw waves
    ctx.beginPath();
    ctx.moveTo(0, canvas.height / 2);
    for (let x = 0; x < canvas.width; x += 10) {
        let y =
            simplex.noise2D(x * noiseScale, time) * waveHeight +
            canvas.height / 2;
        ctx.lineTo(x, y);
    }

    ctx.lineTo(canvas.width, canvas.height);
    ctx.lineTo(0, canvas.height);
    ctx.closePath();

    ctx.fillStyle = "rgba(0, 51, 102, 0.7)";
    ctx.fill();

    // Update time for animation
    time += speed;
}
```

Imagine you have a drawing board in front of you. Before you start creating anything new, you need to erase what's already there, giving yourself a clean slate. This is what ctx.clearRect(0, 0, canvas.width, canvas.height); does. It clears the entire drawing board (or canvas), removing any previous drawings or marks.

Next, you want to set a background color for the canvas. To do this, you set the fill color with ctx.fillStyle = "#f9f9f9";. This line of code tells the computer to use a light grey color. Then, you paint the entire canvas with this color using ctx.fillRect(0, 0, canvas.width, canvas.height), giving you a clean and colored background to start your drawing on.

Now, let's get creative and draw some wavy lines on the canvas to make it more interesting. To start, you tell the computer you're about to draw something new with ctx.beginPath();. It indicates the beginning of a new path or shape to be drawn. Then, you position your drawing tool at a specific point on the canvas using ctx.moveTo(0, canvas.height / 2);. This places the drawing tool at the left edge of the canvas, halfway down from the top.

From here, you begin drawing your wavy lines. You go through each horizontal position on the canvas (from left to right) in steps of 10 pixels using for (let x = 0; x < canvas.width; x += 10). This means that starting from the left edge (x = 0), you move 10 pixels to the right each step until you reach the right edge of the canvas. For each position, you calculate the height of the wave at that point using a noise function. The noise function helps create natural-looking waves, making them appear more random and less uniform.

This calculation is done with let y = simplex.noise2D(x * noiseScale, time) * waveHeight + canvas.height / 2;. Here, simplex.noise2D generates a noise value based on the current x position and time, scaled by a factor noiseScale to control the frequency of the waves. The result is multiplied by waveHeight to set the wave amplitude, and then adjusted vertically to position the wave in the middle of the canvas. Once you know the height of the wave at each position, you draw a line to that point with ctx.lineTo(x, y);. This command creates a line from the current drawing position to the point (x, y). You continue this process for every horizontal position until you reach the end of the canvas.

After drawing all the wavy lines, you close the shape to make it look like a continuous wave with ctx.lineTo(canvas.width, canvas.height); ctx.lineTo(0, canvas.height); ctx.closePath();. These lines of code draw lines from the last point on the wave to the bottom right corner of the canvas, then to the bottom left corner, and finally close the path, completing the shape.

Now that you've outlined your waves, you want to fill them with color to make them visible. You pick a color using ctx.fillStyle =

"rgba(0, 51, 102, 0.7)";. This sets a semi-transparent blue color. Then, you fill the shape with this color using ctx.fill();. This command fills the interior of the path with the selected color.

Finally, to create an animation effect and make the waves appear to move, you update a variable called time by adding a small amount each time you draw a new frame with time += speed;. This makes your waves look like they're in motion because the noise function will generate slightly different values each frame, shifting the wave positions over time. This continuous updating of the time variable creates the illusion of moving waves, bringing your canvas to life.

```
// Resize canvas when window resizes
window.addEventListener("resize", function () {
    canvas.width = window.innerWidth;
    canvas.height = window.innerHeight;
});

// Start animation
animate();
```

Let's talk about how we can make our canvas responsive and continuously animated. Here's what we do:

We want our canvas to adjust itself whenever the browser window is resized. To do this, we set up a system that watches for changes in the window size. So, we create an event listener that's constantly checking for any resizing actions in the browser.

Inside the function we defined for the resize event listener, we have code that changes the size of our canvas to match the new size of the window. This is done using the canvas.width and canvas. height properties. So, whenever the window is resized, the canvas size is updated accordingly. Now that we have a dynamically resizing canvas, we want to start animating it immediately when the page loads and continue the animation smoothly thereafter. To do this, we call a function called animate() that we've defined earlier. This function sets up a loop using requestAnimationFrame, which continuously updates the canvas.

We're gonna ensure that the canvas dynamically resizes with the browser window and starts the animation immediately when the page loads. The resize event listener updates the canvas size whenever the window is resized, maintaining a full-window drawing area. The animate function is called to start the continuous drawing process, creating a smooth, animated wave effect on the canvas.

And there you go, you've just completed the process of creating your first Simplex noise animation, a significant milestone in your journey. Now, let's shift our focus to another important tool that we'll be using for our main animation: the dat.GUI library.

NOTE:

To view your project while you're working on it, you can use an extension called Live Server. You can find and install this extension from the VS Code extensions tab. Live Server will enable you to see your project live as you code, making it easier to see changes in real time.

dat.gui Library

The dat.gui library is a lightweight JavaScript library that provides a simple yet powerful interface for creating graphical user interfaces (GUIs) to control parameters in real time. Developed by Google Chrome Labs, dat.gui allows developers to create interactive controls such as sliders, buttons, and checkboxes with minimal setup.

In our project, we leverage dat.gui to empower users to interactively control various parameters of our emojis, such as speed and size. By incorporating dat.gui into our project, we enable users to customize their emoji experience to suit their preferences, enhancing engagement and interactivity.

Here are a few basic examples of animations using dat.GUI:

Example 1: Animating a Square's Position

Alright, let's dive into creating a simple animation. Imagine you have a canvas, like a blank sheet of paper, where you want to draw something moving. We're going to start with a square. Picture it as a little block.

First off, think about how you'd want it to move. Let's say we want it to slide from left to right across the canvas, like a little square going for a stroll. To make this happen, we're going to need some code, like a set of instructions for the computer to follow.

```html
<!DOCTYPE html>
<html lang="en">
  <head>
    <meta charset="UTF-8" />
    <meta name="viewport" content="width=device-width, initial-scale=1.0" />
    <script src="https://cdnjs.cloudflare.com/ajax/libs/dat-gui/0.7.7/dat.gui.min.js"></script>
    <title>dat.GUI Animation Example #1</title>
    <style>
      body {
        margin: 0;
      }

      canvas {
        display: block;
      }
    </style>
  </head>
  <body>
    <script src="index.js"></script>
  </body>
</html>
```

The HTML document starts with the standard declaration and specifies the language. In the head section, it defines the character encoding and sets the viewport to ensure the website is responsive on various devices.

There's also an important script tag that imports dat.GUI from a CDN, which provides the functionality for our GUI controls. Additionally, a style block is included to remove the default margin of the body and ensure the canvas element displays as a block, allowing it to take up the entire screen smoothly.

```javascript
// Canvas setup
const canvas = document.createElement('canvas');
document.body.appendChild(canvas);
const ctx = canvas.getContext('2d');
canvas.width = window.innerWidth;
canvas.height = window.innerHeight;
```

Imagine you have a blank sheet of paper, which is like a canvas in the digital world. This canvas is like a hidden piece of paper stored in your computer's memory. Now, we want to bring that canvas onto our webpage, just like placing a physical sheet of paper on a table. To start drawing on this canvas, we need to equip ourselves with the right tools. Think of it as getting your paint brushes and colors ready.

To do this, we need to get what's called a "2D drawing context" for our canvas. This context provides us with all the tools and options we need to draw shapes, lines, colors, and more on our canvas. It's like having a full set of painting supplies at our disposal. Next, we want our canvas to fit nicely within the browser window. So, we adjust the width of our canvas to match the width of the browser window. This ensures that our canvas covers the entire width of what's visible in the browser.

Similarly, we adjust the height of our canvas to match the height of the browser window. This ensures that our canvas covers the full height of what's visible in the browser. It's like resizing our canvas to perfectly fit the available space, so we have a large, blank canvas ready for our artistic creations!

```
// Animation variables
let square = {
    x: 50,
    y: canvas.height / 2,
    size: 50,
    speed: 5
};
```

Imagine we have a square on a canvas, like a piece of paper where we can draw things. We're going to control how this square moves.

- **Horizontal Position (x):** This tells us where the square is horizontally on the canvas, like its left-right position. Right now, it's set to 50, so the square is placed 50 pixels from the left edge of the canvas.

- **Vertical Position (y):** This tells us where the square is vertically on the canvas, like its up-down position. By setting it to canvas.height / 2, we're placing the square right in the middle vertically. It ensures the square is centered up and down.

- **Size:** This property simply determines how big the square is. At a size of 50, the square is 50 pixels wide and 50 pixels tall, making it a nice, equal-sized square.

- **Speed:** This is where the animation comes to life! Speed controls how fast the square moves across the screen. With a speed of 5, the square will shift 5 pixels to the right (in the positive x-direction) every time we refresh the screen. So, it's like the square is sliding to the right at a moderate pace, creating the illusion of motion.

```
// dat.GUI setup
const gui = new dat.GUI();
gui.add(square, 'y', 0, canvas.height).name('Position');
gui.add(square, 'size', 10, 100).name('Size');
gui.add(square, 'speed', 1, 10).name('Speed');
```

We're setting up a visual interface to control the animation of a square on a canvas. Think of it like adjusting settings on a dashboard to change how the square moves and looks.

Firstly, we'll setup dat.GUI & create interactive controls. These controls will allow us to adjust various aspects of an animation we're creating. One of the controls we're adding is a slider. This slider lets us change the vertical position (up and down) of a square on a canvas. We can slide it from 0 to the height of the canvas, which gives us a visual representation of where the square is placed vertically.

Next, we're adding another control, which is a slider for changing the size of the square. This slider allows us to adjust the size dynamically, meaning we can make the square smaller or larger as we like. The size range we've set is from 10 to 100 pixels, giving us a good range of flexibility in designing how the square looks.

Lastly, we're introducing a slider to control the speed at which the square moves. This slider lets us change how fast the square moves across the screen. We can adjust the speed from 1 to 10 units per animation frame, allowing us to control the pace of the animation. Each of these controls is labeled clearly using the "name()" method. This makes it easy for us to understand what each control does. With these controls in place, we can adjust the square's position, size, and speed to create the animation effect we want.

```
// Animation Loop
function animate() {
    ctx.clearRect(0, 0, canvas.width, canvas.height);

    // Update square position
    square.x += square.speed;
    if (square.x > canvas.width) square.x = 0;

    // Draw square
    ctx.fillStyle = 'blue';
    ctx.fillRect(square.x, square.y - square.size / 2, square.size, square.size);

    requestAnimationFrame(animate);
}

animate();
```

When creating animations in a web browser, it's essential to manage what's shown on the screen from frame to frame. To achieve this, we often clear the canvas completely at the start of each animation frame. This ensures that remnants of previous frames don't clutter up the current one.

Now, imagine we have a square on our canvas that we want to move horizontally. To do this, we increment the square's x-coordinate by its speed property. This simple action makes the square shift smoothly from left to right. But what happens when our square reaches the right edge of the canvas? We don't want it to disappear instead, we want it to reappear on the left edge, creating an illusion of endless movement. That's where the conditional statement comes in. It checks if the square has reached the canvas's right edge. If it has, it resets the square's x-coordinate to the left edge, ensuring seamless movement.

To make our square visually appealing, we give it a blue color. This makes it stand out against the canvas background. Then, using the fillRect() method, we draw the square at its current position with dimensions specified by its size property. To keep the animation running smoothly, we utilize the requestAnimationFrame() method. This function essentially tells the browser to call our animation function again for the next frame, ensuring a continuous and fluid animation experience for the viewer.

Congratulations on mastering the animation of a square's position! Now that you've accomplished that, let's embark on another exciting adventure into the world of dat.gui & Three.js. This time, we'll dive into a complex yet equally fascinating project.

Example 2: Animating a Spinning Cube

In this example, we'll be exploring the power of dat.GUI combined with the incredible capabilities of Three.js to create captivating visuals right in your web browser. Imagine a canvas where you can sculpt dynamic shapes, manipulate them with the touch of a button and watch them dance in response to your commands.

```
<!DOCTYPE html>
<html lang="en">
  <head>
    <meta charset="UTF-8" />
    <meta name="viewport" content="width=device-width, initial-scale=1.0" />
    <script src="https://cdnjs.cloudflare.com/ajax/libs/three.js/r128/three.min.js"></script>
    <script src="https://cdnjs.cloudflare.com/ajax/libs/dat-gui/0.7.9/dat.gui.min.js"></script>
    <title>dat.GUI Animation Example #2</title>
    <style>
      body {
        margin: 0;
      }

      canvas {
        display: block;
      }
    </style>
  </head>
  <body>
    <script src="index.js"></script>
  </body>
</html>
```

Let's set the stage. Our canvas awaits, nestled within the code you see above. It's a blank slate, ready to be adorned with the magic of motion and interactivity.

We've included the necessary libraries Three.js for rendering our 3D graphics and dat.GUI for effortlessly controlling our animations. These libraries are the paintbrushes and palette for our digital canvas. Also, we're sticking with the same styling as before.

```
// Set up scene, camera, and renderer
const scene = new THREE.Scene();
const camera = new THREE.PerspectiveCamera(75, window.innerWidth / window.innerHeight, 0.1, 1000);
const renderer = new THREE.WebGLRenderer();
renderer.setSize(window.innerWidth, window.innerHeight);
document.body.appendChild(renderer.domElement);
```

We'll start by setting the stage for some visual magic using THREE.js, a powerful JavaScript library for creating 3D content in the browser.

Picture this: a blank canvas waiting to be filled with stunning landscapes, models, or captivating animations. Our stage is represented by a scene, a virtual space where all the action happens. Next, we need a lens to capture this world in all its glory. Enter the camera, positioned just right to frame our scene with the perfect perspective. But what good is a scene and a camera without someone to witness the spectacle? That's where the renderer comes in. It's like our trusty messenger, taking the 3D scene and transforming it into pixels on your screen for you to marvel at.

With everything set up scene, camera, and renderer we're ready to bring our 3D dreams to life!

```
// Set background color
scene.background = new THREE.Color(0x1a1a1a);

// Add a cube to the scene
const geometry = new THREE.BoxGeometry();
const material = new THREE.MeshStandardMaterial({
    color: 0x4caf50,
    roughness: 0.5,
    metalness: 0.1
});
const cube = new THREE.Mesh(geometry, material);
scene.add(cube);
```

Let's add some substance to our 3D world! First up, we're setting the backdrop of our scene to a sleek and sophisticated shade with scene.background. It's like painting the walls of our virtual studio, setting the mood for our upcoming masterpiece.

Now, onto the main event: introducing the star of our show, the humble yet versatile box. With THREE.BoxGeometry, we're sculpting a simple but mighty shape that's ready to take on any form we desire. But what's a box without some flair? That's where the magic of materials comes into play. With THREE.MeshStandardMaterial, we're giving our box a splash of color, a touch of roughness, and just a hint of metalness, transforming it from mundane to magnificent.

And voilà! With our geometry and material in place, we summon our creation into existence with THREE.Mesh and add it to our scene. It's like breathing life into our digital creation, ready to dazzle and delight all who behold it.

```
// Add a light source
const ambientLight = new THREE.AmbientLight(0xffffff, 0.5);
scene.add(ambientLight);

const pointLight = new THREE.PointLight(0xffffff, 1);
pointLight.position.set(5, 5, 5);
scene.add(pointLight);
```

Now we're setting up lighting for a Three.js scene to enhance its visual appeal and realism. First, we create an AmbientLight, which acts as a general illumination across the scene, giving a consistent brightness to all objects regardless of their position or orientation. We set its color to white and adjust its intensity to 50% to avoid overwhelming the scene with brightness.

Next, we introduce a PointLight, which emits light from a specific point in the scene, spreading out in all directions. We also set its color to white and its intensity to full power. By positioning this light at coordinates (5, 5, 5), we place it at a particular spot within the 3D space of our scene.

Combining these two types of lights allows for fine-tuning the atmosphere and highlights in our Three.js scenes, adding depth and realism to the visual experience.

```
// Calculate the distance the camera should be to ensure the cube fits within the view
const aspectRatio = window.innerWidth / window.innerHeight;
const cubeDiagonal = Math.sqrt(3 * Math.pow(1, 2));
const fovRadians = camera.fov * (Math.PI / 180);
const cameraDistance = (cubeDiagonal / 2) / Math.tan(fovRadians / 2);
camera.position.z = cameraDistance * aspectRatio;
```

Let's play with perspective! In the vast expanse of our virtual world, understanding the intricacies of camera placement is key to crafting captivating visuals. With a few mathematical maneuvers, we're about to position our camera just right for an immersive experience.

First off, we calculate the aspect ratio, which is simply the width of our viewport divided by its height. It's like ensuring our camera sees the world in the right proportions, fitting everything perfectly into the frame. Next, we determine the diagonal length of our cube using a bit of geometry magic. Think of it as measuring from one corner to the opposite, capturing the full extent of our 3D object.

Now, armed with the field of view (FOV) in radians, we embark on a journey to find the ideal distance for our camera. By leveraging trigonometry, we calculate the distance based on half the diagonal of our cube and the tangent of half the FOV.

With our calculations complete, we set the camera's position along the z-axis, ensuring it's perfectly poised to capture the scene in all its glory.

```
// Set up dat.GUI
const gui = new dat.GUI();
const cubeFolder = gui.addFolder('Cube');
const cubePositionFolder = cubeFolder.addFolder('Position');
cubeFolder.add(cube.material, 'wireframe');
cubePositionFolder.add(cube.position, 'x', -5, 5);
cubePositionFolder.add(cube.position, 'y', -5, 5);
cubePositionFolder.add(cube.position, 'z', -5, 5);
cubeFolder.open();
cubePositionFolder.open();
```

With dat.GUI, we're giving ourselves the power to tweak and tune our scene with ease, all through a user-friendly interface.

First, we summon dat.GUI into our virtual realm, a versatile tool that allows us to control parameters and settings in real-time. It's like having a control panel at our fingertips, ready to fine-tune our creation with a simple click and drag. Next, we organize our controls into neat folders for better organization and clarity. Picture it as arranging our tools in a tidy toolbox, making it easy to find what we need when inspiration strikes.

Within the "Cube" folder, we have a set of controls dedicated to our cube, starting with the option to toggle its wireframe mode on and off. It's like giving our cube a whole new look with just the flick of a switch!. Delving deeper, we navigate to the "Position" sub-folder, where we can dynamically adjust the cube's coordinates along the x, y, and z axes.

It's like playing with virtual building blocks, reshaping our scene with every adjustment. And with the folders open by default, our controls are readily accessible, inviting us to unleash our creativity and explore the endless possibilities of our 3D world.

```
// Handle window resize to maintain aspect ratio and camera position
window.addEventListener('resize', () => {
    camera.aspect = window.innerWidth / window.innerHeight;
    camera.updateProjectionMatrix();
    renderer.setSize(window.innerWidth, window.innerHeight);
    const newAspectRatio = window.innerWidth / window.innerHeight;
    camera.position.z = cameraDistance * newAspectRatio;
});
```

Let's make our 3D scene responsive! In a world where devices come in all shapes and sizes, ensuring our visual masterpiece adapts to any screen is crucial. Here's how we achieve that: We start by adding an event listener for the resize event on the window. This means our code will spring into action whenever the browser window is resized, keeping our scene looking sharp and well-proportioned.

First, we update the camera's aspect ratio to match the new dimensions of the window. This is like adjusting the lens of a camera to ensure it captures the full picture, no matter the size of the screen. Next, we call camera.updateProjectionMatrix(). This step recalculates the camera's projection matrix, ensuring our 3D scene is rendered correctly with the updated aspect ratio.

Think of it as fine-tuning the camera's settings for the perfect shot. We then adjust the renderer's size to match the new window dimensions. This ensures our entire scene is rendered at the correct resolution, avoiding any stretched or squished visuals. Finally, we recalculate the camera's position along the z-axis, using the updated aspect ratio. This ensures our camera maintains the appropriate distance from the scene, preserving the correct perspective and scale

With these adjustments in place, our 3D scene will seamlessly adapt to any screen size, providing a consistent and immersive experience whether you're on a desktop, tablet, or smartphone.

```
// Animation Loop
function animate() {
    requestAnimationFrame(animate);

    // Add rotation for a smooth animation
    cube.rotation.x += 0.01;
    cube.rotation.y += 0.01;

    renderer.render(scene, camera);
}

animate();
```

Let's make our 3D scene come alive with a continuous and smooth animation! By defining an animate function, we're setting up an infinite loop that will keep our cube rotating and our scene dynamically engaging. We start with the animate function. This function will be called repeatedly to update our scene and render the changes. Inside the animate function, we call requestAnimationFrame(animate). This method tells the browser to call the animate function before the next repaint.

It's an efficient way to create smooth animations by leveraging the browser's native refresh rate. We update the cube's rotation on the x and y axes by a small amount (0.01). This gradual change will create a smooth spinning effect. After updating the cube's rotation, we call renderer.render(scene, camera) to draw the current state of the scene. This step updates the display to reflect the changes made in this frame.

Finally, we call the animate function once to kick off the animation loop.

And there you go, you've mastered the art of creating complex animations using dat.GUI and ThreeJS. Now it's time to put those skills to use and start crafting some expressive emojis. Let's dive in and bring those emojis to life with vibrant, dynamic movements.

***

Here are some challenges where you can put your learnings into practice:

1. Basic Emoji Display

Objective: Integrate a simple emoji into an HTML page.

Task:

- Create a new HTML file.
- Add the basic HTML structure (<!DOCTYPE html>, <html>, <head>, <body>).
- Inside the <body>, use the <span> element to display an emoji of your choice.

2. Random Emoji Placement

Objective: Use the Simplex Noise Library to place emojis randomly on the screen.

Task:

- Include the Simplex Noise library in your HTML file.
- Generate random coordinates using Simplex Noise.
- Place multiple emojis at these coordinates.

3. Interactive Emoji Size

Objective: Use dat.GUI to create an interactive control that changes the size of an emoji.

Task:

- Include the dat.GUI library in your HTML file.
- Create a GUI with a slider to adjust the emoji size.
- Apply the size change to the emoji.

Chapter 3

CSS Styling & Page Optimization

When it comes to crafting captivating websites, every designer understands the paramount importance of CSS (Cascading Style Sheets) in shaping the visual appeal and functionality of a webpage.

CSS is the backbone of web design, allowing designers to control everything from fonts and colors to layout and positioning.

However, CSS rendering can sometimes behave unexpectedly due to default browser styles, leading to inconsistencies across different platforms. Each web browser has its own default style settings, which can affect how elements are displayed. For example, the default margin and padding of an element in Chrome may differ from those in Firefox or Safari. These discrepancies can cause significant variations in the appearance of a webpage, making it look different from one browser to another. This lack of uniformity can be particularly frustrating for web designers who strive for precision and consistency in their designs.

This is where CSS reset comes into play, offering a solution to standardize the styling across various browsers and ensure a consistent user experience.

Q. What is CSS Reset?

A CSS Reset is a tool that helps web developers get rid of the default styles applied by browsers to HTML elements. These built-in styles can be different across various browsers, causing inconsistencies in how web pages look. By using a CSS reset, developers can start with a clean slate, making it easier to achieve a consistent appearance across all browsers.

Browsers automatically apply their own styles when loading a webpage, affecting things like headings, lists, and form fields. These variations can be annoying for developers who want a uniform design.

A CSS reset neutralizes these default styles, creating a blank canvas. This allows developers to have precise control over the styling of each element on the page.

With this clean starting point, developers can apply their own styles without the default browser styles getting in the way, ensuring their design looks the same on all browsers.

In short, a CSS reset is essential in modern web development. It provides a consistent foundation for styling web pages, helps avoid browser-specific issues, and ensures that designs appear as intended on any device or browser.

By removing the unpredictable nature of default browser styles, a CSS reset allows for a more controlled and uniform web design process.

1. Basic Reset Example:

```css
/* Resetting margins, padding, and borders */
* {
  margin: 0;
  padding: 0;
  box-sizing: border-box;
}

/* Setting a consistent font family and size */
body {
  font-family: Arial, sans-serif;
  font-size: 16px;
}
```

In this example, the * selector resets the margin, padding, and border of all elements to zero, ensuring a uniform starting point. The box-sizing: border-box property makes it easier to work with widths and heights.

Additionally, setting a consistent font family and size in the body tag ensures that all text appears the same across different browsers.

2. HTML Reset Example:

In this example, we'll see how to reset the styles for HTML5 elements, ensuring they all display as block elements by default.

We'll start by setting elements like <header>, <section>, <article>, and <aside> to display as block elements, guaranteeing they take up the full width available. Next, we'll remove default list styles for <ol> and <ul> to eliminate default bullets, numbers, and spacing, allowing for custom styling.

Lastly, we'll ensure images scale properly within their containers by setting their maximum width to 100%, maintaining aspect ratio and preventing overflow issues.

```css
/* Resetting styles for HTML5 elements */
article,
details,
footer,
header,
main,
nav,
section,
summary {
  display: block;
}

/* Removing default list styles */
ol,
ul {
  list-style: none;
}

/* Ensuring images scale properly */
img {
  max-width: 100%;
  height: auto;
}
```

In this CSS reset, we first ensure that the specified HTML5 elements are treated as block-level elements. Next, we remove the default list styles for ordered and unordered lists by setting their list-style, margin, and padding to none and zero, respectively.

Finally, we ensure that images are responsive by setting their max-width to 100% and their height to auto. This approach guarantees that images will scale appropriately within their containers, maintaining their aspect ratio and preventing overflow issues.

Understanding the Code:

```
body,
html {
  margin: 0;
  padding: 0;
  width: 100%;
  height: 100%;
  overflow: hidden;
}
```

Body, HTML Selector

The body, html selector commands immediate attention, as it encapsulates two fundamental entities essential to the architecture of a webpage: the <body> and <html> elements. These elements serve as the cornerstone upon which the entire structure of a webpage is constructed. Within the realm of web development, the body, html selector holds significant sway, offering developers a powerful directive to synchronize their presentation efforts seamlessly. It establishes the foundational framework necessary for a cohesive and aesthetically pleasing layout to emerge.

The <html> element represents the root of an HTML document, encompassing all other elements within its domain. It serves as the container for crucial metadata, document-wide settings, and other essential information. Meanwhile, the <body> element defines the content area of the webpage, encompassing all visible elements that users interact with. It acts as the canvas upon which developers paint their digital creations, housing textual content, images, multimedia, and interactive elements.

By employing the body, html selector, developers are empowered to orchestrate these foundational elements in unison, ensuring a harmonious and structured presentation.

This directive serves as a guiding force, enabling developers to establish a solid groundwork from which to build engaging and user-friendly web experiences

Zeroing In on Margins and Padding

Once the foundational elements of a webpage are set, the next step is to fine-tune margins and padding. By declaring margin: 0; padding: 0;, developers effectively remove any default spacing that might linger throughout the webpage.

This careful intervention serves a dual purpose: firstly, it creates a clean canvas ready for design enhancements, and secondly, it ensures a consistent user experience across different web browsers.

In essence, adjusting margins and padding meticulously not only enhances the visual presentation of the webpage but also demonstrates a commitment to providing a cohesive and smooth browsing experience for users, no matter which platform or browser they use.

Expanding to Full Coverage

With the canvas meticulously prepared, the next directive invites the webpage to extend its reach to the farthest bounds. By invoking the commands width: 100%; height: 100%;, the developer grants the page the authority to command the entirety of the viewport.

In this transformative act, the webpage ascends to a state of transcendence, eradicating any traces of vacant space and enveloping the viewer within its immersive embrace. This approach not only expands the visual expanse of the webpage but also ensures that every pixel of the viewport is utilized to its fullest potential. Consequently, it enhances user engagement and fosters a deeper connection with the content.

By embracing full coverage, the webpage goes beyond just filling the screen. It transforms into a captivating digital tableau that truly engages and enthrals its audience.

Concealing the Overflow

This property acts as a vigilant guardian, ensuring that any content attempting to overflow its designated space is promptly hidden. By doing so, scroll bars are eliminated, preserving the clean and polished look of the webpage.

By concealing overflow, this property maintains the integrity of the webpage's layout, preventing any disruptive elements from disrupting the carefully crafted design. It upholds a sense of cohesion and order, presenting the content in a way that is both visually pleasing and easy to navigate.

Benefits of CSS Reset:

Consistency

One of the primary benefits of CSS reset lies in its ability to promote consistency across different web browsers. In the absence of a reset, browsers apply their default styles to HTML elements, leading to variations in appearance across platforms. These discrepancies can disrupt the visual identity that developers aim to achieve. By implementing a CSS reset, developers effectively neutralize the influence of browser-specific styles, establishing a uniform baseline from which to build upon.

This uniformity ensures that the design remains consistent, regardless of the browser used by the viewer, thereby enhancing the overall user experience.

Predictability

CSS reset empowers developers with a sense of predictability in their styling endeavours. When starting with a clean slate, free from the influence of browser defaults, developers can anticipate how their styles will be applied across different platforms. This predictability eliminates the risk of unexpected browser interference, allowing developers to execute their creative vision with confidence.

By establishing a standardized starting point, CSS reset provides a level of control and predictability that is essential for crafting polished and cohesive web designs.

Ease of Maintenance

Maintaining a website's design integrity is a continuous endeavour, often requiring updates and refinements over time. CSS reset plays a crucial role in easing the maintenance burden placed on developers. By adhering to a standardized baseline, updating styles becomes more straightforward and less prone to compatibility issues. Designers can make modifications confidently, knowing that the reset ensures consistency and compatibility across browsers. This streamlined approach to maintenance not only saves time and effort but also contributes to the longevity of the design's effectiveness.

Improved Cross-Browser Compatibility

In today's diverse digital landscape, where users access websites from a multitude of devices and browsers, achieving cross-browser compatibility is paramount. CSS reset serves as a powerful tool for mitigating the differences in default styles among browsers, thereby fostering a more harmonious browsing experience for users. By neutralizing browser-specific quirks and inconsistencies, CSS reset ensures that the design remains visually cohesive and functional across various platforms. This improved compatibility enhances accessibility and usability, ultimately contributing to the success of the website.

CSS reset offers numerous advantages, including consistency, predictability, simplified maintenance, and enhanced cross-browser compatibility. It empowers developers to create visually appealing and user-friendly web experiences with confidence, ensuring seamless resonance across digital platforms.

***

Here are some challenges where you can put your learnings into practice:

1. Implementing a Basic CSS Reset

Objective: Apply a basic CSS Reset to an HTML page.

Task:

- Create a new HTML file.
- Add the basic HTML structure (<!DOCTYPE html>, <html>, <head>, <body>).
- In the <head>, include a <style> block with a simple CSS Reset.

2. Customize a CSS Reset

Objective: Customize a CSS Reset to suit your own preferences

Task:

- Create a new HTML file.
- Add a basic CSS Reset in the <head>.
- Customize the reset to include additional styles, such as setting a default font or background color.

3. Animated Emoji with CSS

Objective: Create an animated emoji using CSS.

Task:

- Use the HTML file from Chp 2.
- Add a <style> block in the <head> section.
- Apply a CSS animation to the emoji to make it bounce & add it to the center of the page.

Chapter 4

Interactive Emoji Magic with JavaScript

Understanding Constants in JavaScript

In JavaScript, a constant is a variable whose value cannot be changed once it has been assigned. This concept is particularly useful when dealing with values that should remain constant throughout the execution of a program. JavaScript does have built-in support for constants using the const keyword.

While it's common practice to use uppercase identifiers for constants in many programming languages, including JavaScript, the const keyword explicitly enforces immutability by preventing reassignment.

Declaring Constants

Constants are declared using the const keyword followed by the identifier and an assignment of a value. The syntax is straightforward. In this example, PI is a constant representing the mathematical constant π. Any attempt to reassign a value to PI will result in a TypeError.

```
const PI = 3.14159;
```

Immutability and Reassignment

The defining characteristic of a constant in JavaScript is its immutability. Once a constant is assigned a value, it cannot be reassigned:

```
const MAX_USERS = 100;
MAX_USERS = 200; // TypeError: Assignment to constant variable.
```

This immutability guarantees that the value of MAX_USERS remains 100, preventing accidental changes that could lead to bugs or inconsistent program behaviour.

Scope of Constants

Constants, like variables declared with let, are block-scoped. This means they are only accessible within the block they are defined in:

```
if (true) {
    const GREETING = 'Hello World!';
    console.log(GREETING); // Outputs: Hello World!
}
console.log(GREETING); // ReferenceError: GREETING is not defined
```

The constant GREETING is only accessible within the if block. Outside of this block, attempting to access GREETING will result in a ReferenceError.

Best Practices for Constants

While JavaScript does not enforce any specific naming convention for constants, it is common practice to use uppercase identifiers with underscores to separate words.

This convention helps distinguish constants from regular variables and improve code readability:

```
const MAX_HEIGHT = 250;
const API_KEY = '12345-ABCDE';
```

Adhering to this convention makes it clear that MAX_HEIGHT and API_KEY are constants, indicating their values should not be altered.

Constants with Complex Data Types

It is crucial to understand that the immutability of constants applies to the variable binding, not the value itself. For objects and arrays, the reference to the object or array cannot be changed, but the contents can still be modified:

```
const USER = { name: 'John Doe', age: 30 };
USER.age = 31; // This is allowed
USER = { name: 'Jane Doe', age: 25 }; // TypeError: Assignment to constant variable.
```

In this example, while the USER constant cannot be reassigned to a new object, the properties of the object it references can be modified.

Therefore, it is essential to understand the distinction between the immutability of the reference and the mutability of the value the reference points to.

```
const PI = Math.PI;
const TAU = 2 * PI;
```

In our code, the mathematical constant PI, denoted by the symbol π, represents the ratio of a circle's circumference to its diameter. In JavaScript, you can access the value of PI through the Math.PI property. It is approximately equal to 3.14159, though JavaScript provides a more accurate representation.

TAU is a lesser-known mathematical constant, representing the ratio of a circle's circumference to its radius. It is essentially equal to 2 times PI.

While not as commonly used as PI, TAU offers certain advantages in mathematical calculations, particularly in contexts where the use of radians is prevalent. In JavaScript, you can leverage these constants in calculations involving circles, angles, and other geometric operations.

Additionally, they can enhance the precision and readability of your code, making it easier to understand and maintain.

Best Practices

When working with constants in JavaScript, it's crucial to follow certain best practices to ensure code clarity and maintainability. Here are some guidelines to follow:

Use Descriptive Names: Choose meaningful and descriptive names for your constants that accurately convey their purpose or value. This makes it easier for other developers (and your future self) to understand their significance without needing to refer back to the code.

Adhere to Naming Conventions: Follow established naming conventions for constants, such as using uppercase letters and underscores to separate words (e.g., MY_CONSTANT_VALUE). Consistency in naming helps maintain a uniform coding style throughout your project.

Document Usage: Document the purpose and usage of each constant within your codebase. You can do this through comments or inline documentation, providing context for why the constant is used and any constraints or considerations associated with it.

Group Related Constants: Group related constants together, either within the same file or in dedicated modules, to keep them organized and easily accessible. This improves code readability and helps developers locate relevant constants when making changes or debugging.

Avoid Magic Numbers and Strings: Refrain from using "magic" numbers or strings directly in your code. Instead, define them as constants with descriptive names to enhance code readability and make it easier to update values in the future.

Use Constants for Configuration: Use constants to store configuration values or settings that may change over time, such as API endpoints, timeout durations, or feature toggles. This centralizes configuration management and makes it simpler to modify settings across your application.

By following these best practices, you can streamline your development process, enhance code clarity, and facilitate collaboration with other developers working on the same codebase. Additionally, well-documented and properly named constants contribute to the maintainability and scalability of your JavaScript projects over time.

Drawing with Canvas in JavaScript

Canvas is a powerful HTML element that allows for dynamic, scriptable rendering of 2D shapes and bitmap images. Now we'll learn how to use the canvas element in conjunction with JavaScript to draw emojis on a web page.

```
const canvas = document.querySelector(".emojis");
const ctx = canvas.getContext("2d");
```

In this code, we first select the canvas element from the HTML document using the querySelector method. The .emojis class is used to uniquely identify the canvas element. Once the canvas element is selected, we obtain its rendering context using the getContext method with the argument "2d", indicating a two-dimensional drawing context.

The rendering context, represented by the variable ctx, provides methods and properties that allow us to draw and manipulate graphics within the canvas. The "2d" context is suitable for creating 2D graphics, including shapes, text, images, and more.

With the rendering context initialized, we can now start drawing on the canvas. Here are some common drawing operations:

- **Lines:** Use methods like moveTo and lineTo to draw straight lines.

```
const canvas = document.getElementById('canvas');
const ctx = canvas.getContext('2d');

ctx.beginPath();
ctx.moveTo(50, 50);
ctx.lineTo(200, 50);
ctx.stroke();
```

- **Rectangles**: Create rectangles using fillRect or strokeRect.

```
ctx.fillStyle = 'brown';
ctx.fillRect(50, 50, 100, 100);
```

- **Circles:** Draw circles using arc method.

```
ctx.beginPath();
ctx.arc(100, 100, 50, 0, 2 * Math.PI);
ctx.fill(); // Can also add ctx.stroke()
```

- **Adding the Text:** Use the fillText or strokeText methods to add text to the canvas.

```
ctx.font = '30px Arial';
ctx.fillText('Hello World', 50, 50);
```

- **Styling and Color:** Set the stroke and fill styles using strokeStyle and fillStyle & define colors using CSS color values or RGBA values.

```
ctx.fillStyle = 'green';
ctx.strokeStyle = 'red';
ctx.lineWidth = 5;

ctx.fillRect(50, 50, 100, 100);
ctx.strokeRect(50, 50, 100, 100);
```

- **Image Manipulation:** Load images onto the canvas using the drawImage method. It's essential to consider the size and resolution of the canvas. The default size of a canvas is 300 pixels wide and 150 pixels high, but you can adjust it using the width and height attributes or CSS styles.

```
const img = new Image();
img.onLoad = function() {
  ctx.drawImage(img, 50, 50); // CAN ADJUST THE POSITION & SIZE OF THE IMAGE
}
img.src = 'example.jpg'; // CAN ADD YOUR IMAGE HERE...
```

Exploring Emoji Art with JavaScript: A Visual Journey

In the digital age, communication has transcended traditional text to include a vibrant array of emojis, adding depth and expression to our interactions. JavaScript, a versatile programming language, offers a canvas for creativity through emoji art.

Now, we'll embark on a journey to explore the fusion of coding and artistry, using JavaScript to animate an array of emojis.

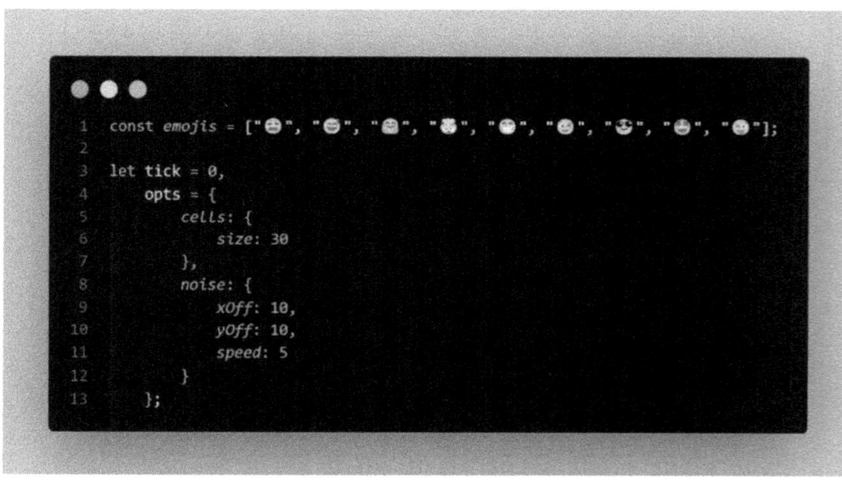

Our adventure begins with the foundation: setting up our environment. We define an array called 'emojis', housing a selection of expressive characters that will bring our art to life. Each emoji carries its own personality, from laughter to surprise, ensuring a dynamic visual experience. With our emojis ready, we create a canvas using JavaScript, providing a digital space for our artistry to unfold- Through the manipulation of parameters such as cell size, we mold the canvas to suit our vision, laying the groundwork for the magic to come. Emojis are not static, they pulsate with energy and emotion. By controlling noise variables such as xOff, yOff, and speed, we simulate dynamic shifts, imbuing our emojis with a sense of life.

Unveiling the Simplex Noise: A Gateway to Dynamic Creations

In the realm of computer graphics and procedural generation, noise plays a crucial role in creating natural-looking textures, terrain, and patterns. Among various noise algorithms, Simplex Noise stands out for its efficiency, visual quality, and ease of implementation.

Simplex Noise, developed by Ken Perlin in 2001 as an improvement over his earlier Perlin Noise algorithm, is a method for generating noise in multiple dimensions. Unlike Perlin Noise, which operates in three-dimensional space, Simplex Noise works in any number of dimensions, making it versatile for various applications.

```
const simplex = new SimplexNoise();
```

In JavaScript, the const keyword is employed to declare a constant variable, ensuring that its value remains unchanged throughout the program.

In our context, simplex serves as the moniker for our Simplex Noise object, allowing for seamless identification within the codebase. Utilizing the new keyword, we initiate the creation of a fresh instance belonging to the SimplexNoise class. This action, facilitated by the SimplexNoise() function call, instantiates an object ready to deliver the intricate functionalities encapsulated within the Simplex Noise algorithm.

The SimplexNoise() function typically belongs to a library or module (which we have declared in the HTML File) that implements the Simplex Noise algorithm. When called with new, it returns a new instance of the SimplexNoise class, which encapsulates the necessary functions and data structures to generate simplex noise.

***

Here are some challenges where you can put your learnings into practice:

1. Defining & Using Constants

Objective: Learn how to define and use constants in JavaScript.

Task:

- Create a new HTML file with a <script> block.
- Define a constant for an emoji and display it in an alert.

2. Draw an emoji on Canvas

Objective: Draw an emoji on a canvas element using JavaScript.

Task:

- Create a new HTML file with a <canvas> element.
- Use JavaScript to draw an emoji inside the canvas.

3. Create Emoji Patterns

Objective: Use JavaScript to create a pattern of emojis on the canvas

Task:

- Create a new HTML file with a <canvas> element.
- Use JavaScript to draw a grid of emojis on the canvas.

4. Generating Random Emoji Positions with Simplex Noise

Objective: Use Simplex Noise to place emojis randomly on the canvas.

Task:

- Include the Simplex Noise library in your HTML file.
- Use Simplex Noise to generate random coordinates and draw emojis at those positions on the canvas.

Chapter 5

Animating Emojis with JavaScript: Adding Life to Web Interactions

---

In the realm of creating engaging user experiences, the integration of dynamic and interactive elements plays a pivotal role. Among these elements, emojis have emerged as vibrant and expressive characters that infuse web applications with personality and charm.

In this chapter, we delve into the intricacies of animating emojis using JavaScript. We'll delve into the underlying principles and techniques that drive this captivating endeavor, unraveling the secrets behind bringing these beloved symbols to life on the digital canvas.

Introduction To The Emoji Class

The Emoji class serves as the blueprint for creating and managing emojis within our animation. It embodies the essence of each emoji, defining its visual appearance, position, and movement throughout the animation.

```
class Emoji {
    constructor(x, y, size) {
        this.position = { x, y };
        this.size = size;
    }
```

The Emoji class starts with a constructor method, which plays a crucial role in setting up the initial state of the emoji instance. This method is responsible for initializing the emoji with specific coordinates and size parameters. When an emoji object is created, the constructor method assigns values to its x and y coordinates, determining its position on the canvas. Additionally, it sets the size of the emoji, which defines its visual dimensions. By initializing these attributes, the constructor method ensures that each emoji has a unique location and size, forming the basis for its representation on the canvas.

This setup process is essential as it establishes the foundational properties that will dictate how the emoji will appear and be displayed within the graphical environment.

Rendering Emojis with the draw() Method

In the realm of animation, rendering serves as the mechanism through which visual elements are brought to life. Within the Emoji class, the draw() method assumes this pivotal role, orchestrating the rendering process with finesse and precision.

```
draw() {
        let noiseVal = (simplex.noise3D(this.position.x / (opts.noise.xOff * 50), this.position.y / (opts.noise.yOff * 50), tick / (opts.noise.speed * 50)) + 1) / 2;
        ctx.font = `${this.size}px sans-serif`;
        ctx.textBaseline = "middle";
        ctx.textAlign = "center";
        ctx.fillText(emojis[Math.round(noiseVal * 8)], this.position.x, this.position.y);
    }
}
```

The draw() method uses simplex noise to create smooth and natural-looking patterns and textures, giving our emojis dynamic movement. By using this function, we add an element of randomness that makes the animation feel more fluid and organic, moving beyond simple, static images. To really understand the intricacies of our animation, we need to break down the draw() method and take a close look at each part.

Simplex Noise Generation

At the core of our animation lies the magic of simplexnoise3D(), a powerful tool for generating three-dimensional noise. This function opens up a world of possibilities, allowing us to give our emojis a dynamic and constantly changing presence.

By tweaking the parameters of simplex.noise3D() specifically, the x and y coordinates of the emoji along with the current frame count (tick) we can finely control the intensity and direction of their movement. This precise manipulation helps us create fluid, organic motions, bringing our emojis to life in a mesmerizing way.

With each loop of the animation, we dynamically adjust these parameters, harnessing the natural randomness of simplex noise to introduce subtle variations and nuances in the motion. This technique ensures that the animation feels dynamic, natural, and vibrant, capturing the viewer's attention and enhancing their experience.

The use of simplex.noise3D() is fundamental to our animation, allowing us to infuse our emojis with a lively realism that significantly enhances the visual impact of our work.

Text Rendering

With the computed noise value in hand, we embark on the next step: rendering the appropriate emoji onto the canvas. To achieve this, we utilize the ctx.fillText() method, a versatile tool in the canvas API arsenal.

Drawing upon a predefined array of emojis, indexed by the rounded noise value, we ensure that each emoji is imbued with a unique identity reflective of its underlying characteristics. This array acts as a repository of visual representations, allowing us to match the noise value to a specific emoji. By leveraging the ctx.fillText() method, we effectively transfer the selected emoji onto the canvas, positioning it at the designated coordinates.

This process repeats iteratively, with each frame of the animation cycle, resulting in a dynamic and visually engaging sequence.

Font Styling

With great attention to detail, we fine-tune the font styling for each emoji, ensuring precise rendering that enhances the viewer's immersion. Leveraging the canvas API's features such as ctx.font, ctx.textBaseline, and ctx.textAlign, we adjust the font size, baseline alignment, and text alignment.

By setting the ctx.font, we define the size and style of the font used to render the emojis. The ctx.textBaseline property determines the alignment of the text relative to the specified baseline, ensuring consistent vertical positioning.

Additionally, the ctx.textAlign property controls the horizontal alignment of the text within its bounding box, further refining the visual presentation. This font styling process contributes to a cohesive and visually appealing display of emojis, enhancing the viewer's immersion in the animation. User interaction takes center stage in shaping the user experience.

To empower users with the ability to manipulate and customize visual elements dynamically, we turn to dat.GUI, a lightweight and intuitive graphical user interface library.

Introduction to dat.GUI

At the heart of our endeavour lies dat.GUI, a library renowned for its simplicity and ease of integration. By leveraging its interface, we empower users to adjust animation parameters in real-time, fostering a sense of engagement and interactivity.

```
function initializeGUI() {
    let GUI = new dat.GUI();

    let f1 = GUI.addFolder("cells");
    f1.open();
    f1.add(opts.cells, "size").step(1).min(15).max(50);
    let f2 = GUI.addFolder("noise");
    f2.open();
    f2.add(opts.noise, "xOff").step(1).min(1).max(100);
    f2.add(opts.noise, "yOff").step(1).min(1).max(100);
    f2.add(opts.noise, "speed").step(1).min(1).max(100);
}
```

The initialization of dat.GUI begins with the creation of a GUI instance, laying the foundation for interactive control. Following the creation of the GUI instance, we craft the user interface by organizing folders and incorporating individual controls. This structure allows for the seamless navigation and manipulation of settings, ensuring that users can interact with our animation.

Folder Creation

Utilizing the addFolder() method, we establish separate folders, each designated as a container for sets of animation parameters. This practice of encapsulating parameters within logical groupings enhances the navigational structure and organization of the graphical interface, thereby fostering a more intuitive user experience.

By categorizing related parameters into distinct folders, we streamline the accessibility of controls and enhance the overall clarity of the interface. Users can identify and interact with specific sets of parameters, leading to a more efficient and enjoyable interaction with the animation environment.

The strategic use of folders empowers us to structure and present complex animation controls in a manner that is both comprehensible and user-friendly, ultimately elevating the usability and effectiveness of our application. This thoughtful organization ensures that users can navigate and manipulate the animation settings with ease, making the process of customization straightforward and engaging.

Parameter Controls

Within each folder, we introduce parameter controls using the add() method, enabling users to manipulate animation properties with precision and ease. This approach allows us to specify the parameter to be controlled, such as opts.cells.size or opts.noise.xOff, and define constraints regarding its range and granularity. This gives users fine-grained control over the dynamics of the animation.

By providing intuitive controls for adjusting specific parameters, users can tailor the animation experience to their preferences with remarkable precision. Whether it's tweaking the size of individual cells or modulating the horizontal offset of noise patterns, users have the tools necessary to sculpt the animation exactly as they desire.

The incorporation of parameter controls empowers users to engage with the animation environment on a deeper level. It allows them to fine-tune its behavior to align with their creative vision or functional requirements. This level of control enhances the usability and versatility of the application, making for a more immersive and rewarding user experience.

Through these controls, users can explore and customize the animation in ways that make it truly their own, transforming a static experience into an interactive and personalized journey.

Enhancing User Experience

By equipping users with intuitive controls for effortlessly modifying animation parameters, we empower them to become active participants in the creative process. This approach ensures that everyone, regardless of their background or expertise, can engage with the animation interface confidently and easily. At its core, the utilization of dat.GUI serves as a beacon of accessibility and inclusivity, breaking down barriers and fostering a collaborative environment where creativity flourishes.

Whether users are seasoned designers or just exploring the world of web development, they are empowered to shape the animation according to their unique vision and preferences.

With each adjustment made through dat.GUI, users wield the power to breathe life into their ideas and aspirations, transforming them into dynamic and captivating animations. This collaborative interaction between users and the animation interface unlocks a world of endless possibilities, where creativity knows no bounds, and innovation thrives.

The ease and flexibility offered by dat.GUI make the creative process enjoyable and accessible, allowing every user to leave their mark on the animation in meaningful and imaginative ways.

Canvas Crafting: Master the Art of Dynamic Resizing

In the dynamic world of web development, staying adaptable is crucial for delivering top-notch user experiences across different devices and screen sizes. A key aspect of this adaptability lies in our ability to smoothly resize canvas elements using JavaScript. This enables us to cater to a wide range of viewport dimensions with precision and finesse.

By seamlessly adjusting the canvas dimensions based on changes in the viewport size, we empower our creations to effortlessly adapt to various browsing environments. This fosters a unified and immersive user experience, ensuring that our content remains engaging and accessible across the digital landscape.

```
function adjustCanvasSize() {
    canvas.width = window.innerWidth;
    canvas.height = window.innerHeight;
}
```

The adjustCanvasSize() function serves as the linchpin of our canvas resizing strategy, orchestrating the transformation of canvas dimensions with elegance and efficiency.

Let us delve into its inner workings to unravel the mechanisms by which this essential functionality is realized.

Window Dimensions

Through accessing the properties window.innerWidth and window.innerHeight, we acquire real-time measurements of the browser window. These measurements provide valuable insight into the limitations within which our canvas operates.

To elaborate, the canvas element serves as a designated area within a web page where graphics and animations can be rendered dynamically. Its size and position can be controlled via HTML and JavaScript. However, to ensure optimal presentation and functionality, it's crucial to adapt the canvas dimensions to the current dimensions of the user's browser window. The properties window.innerWidth and window.innerHeight facilitate this adaptation by providing accurate measurements of the browser viewport's width and height, respectively. These measurements dynamically reflect any changes made to the browser window size, ensuring that the canvas adjusts accordingly.

By incorporating these real-time measurements into our function, we gain a deeper understanding of the constraints within which our canvas operates. This enables us to create responsive and visually appealing web experiences that seamlessly adapt to varying screen sizes and resolutions.

The utilization of window.innerWidth and window.innerHeight properties within our function enables us to obtain precise measurements of the browser window dimensions, thereby allowing for effective management of canvas size and layout in response to user interactions and device characteristics.

Canvas Resizing

With an understanding of the viewport dimensions, our next step involves resizing the canvas element. This is achieved by adjusting the width and height attributes of the canvas element based on the dimensions of the viewport. By assigning the canvas.width and canvas.height properties to match the viewport dimensions, we ensure that our canvas dynamically expands or contracts, smoothly adapting to fluctuations in screen size.

This fluid resizing process guarantees that the canvas maintains its integrity and visual quality across various devices and screen resolutions. Whether the user is viewing the content on a large desktop monitor or a handheld device, the canvas adjusts seamlessly to provide an optimal viewing experience. By synchronizing the canvas dimensions with those of the viewport, we enhance the responsiveness and versatility of our web application or interactive content. This adaptive approach not only improves user engagement but also demonstrates a commitment to delivering a polished and user-friendly interface.

By aligning the canvas dimensions with the viewport dimensions through the manipulation of canvas.width and canvas.height properties, we achieve a flexible and dynamic canvas layout that responds gracefully to changes in screen size, ensuring a consistent and enjoyable user experience across different devices and viewing environments.

Enabling Responsive Design

The implementation of responsive design through canvas resizing signifies a monumental step forward in our pursuit of a user-centric web experience. Responsive design is an approach dedicated to the seamless adaptation of web content to a wide array of devices and display resolutions, ensuring accessibility and usability for every user, regardless of their device. By leveraging JavaScript to free our canvas from fixed dimensions, we enable it to dynamically adjust its size and layout in response to changes in viewport dimensions.

This dynamic and fluid aesthetic not only enhances visual appeal but also fosters engagement and immersion for users across various platforms.

Responsive design prioritizes inclusivity and user satisfaction, addressing the diverse needs and preferences of our audience. By thoughtfully implementing responsive principles and paying attention to details, we elevate the user experience, transforming our canvas-based content into a versatile and adaptable medium. This medium resonates with users regardless of the device or screen size they are using, ensuring a consistent and optimized experience.

The strategic utilization of JavaScript in enabling canvas resizing is central to our approach. Instead of adhering to fixed dimensions, JavaScript allows the canvas to respond dynamically to changes in the viewport. This means that whether a user is accessing our content on a desktop monitor, a tablet, or a smartphone, the canvas will adjust accordingly, maintaining the integrity and visual appeal of the content.

For example, on a large desktop screen, the canvas might expand to fill available space, providing a more immersive experience, while on a smaller smartphone screen, it might condense and rearrange elements to ensure readability and usability.

Benefits of Responsive Design:

1. Enhanced User Engagement:

Responsive design ensures that users have a seamless experience, regardless of the device they use. This continuity can lead to increased engagement, as users are more likely to stay on a website that is easy to navigate and visually appealing.

For instance, a user switching from their desktop to their mobile device can continue their browsing without any disruption, leading to a more cohesive and satisfying experience

2. Improved Accessibility:

By adapting to various screen sizes and resolutions, responsive design makes web content more accessible to users with disabilities.

For example, users with visual impairments may rely on larger text sizes or screen readers. Responsive design can accommodate these needs by adjusting text size and layout dynamically.

3. SEO Benefits:

Search engines Favor websites that provide a good user experience, and responsive design is a key factor in this. A mobile-friendly website is more likely to rank higher in search engine results, driving more traffic to the site.

This can be particularly beneficial for businesses looking to increase their online presence and reach a broader audience.

4. Cost-Effectiveness:

Maintaining a single responsive website is more cost-effective than managing multiple versions of a site for different devices. This unified approach reduces development and maintenance costs while ensuring consistency across platforms.

5. Future-Proofing:

As new devices with varying screen sizes and resolutions are released, a responsive design approach ensures that our content remains accessible and visually appealing.

This future-proofs our website, reducing the need for frequent redesigns to accommodate new technology.

Introduction to Emoji Grid Rendering

At the core of our pursuit lies the concept of emoji grid rendering a blend of mathematics and creativity that infuses the canvas with a dynamic mosaic of expressive characters.

By orchestrating the precise placement and rendering of emojis within a structured grid, we craft a visually captivating tableau that captivates the senses and ignites the imagination.

```
function drawEmojiGrid() {
    ctx.fillStyle = "rgb(102, 69, 0)";
    ctx.fillRect(0, 0, canvas.width, canvas.height);

    let x, y, cell;
    const cols = Math.ceil(canvas.width / opts.cells.size);
    const rows = Math.ceil(canvas.height / opts.cells.size);

    for (let i = 0; i < cols; i++) {
        for (let j = 0; j < rows; j++) {
            x = i * opts.cells.size + opts.cells.size / 2;
            y = j * opts.cells.size + opts.cells.size / 2;
            cell = new Emoji(x, y, opts.cells.size);
            cell.draw();
        }
    }
}
```

The drawEmojiGrid() function serves as the backbone of our emoji grid rendering process, orchestrating the placement and rendering of emojis within a structured grid on the canvas.

Let us unravel the intricacies of this essential function.

Background Fill

To create a visually appealing background for our project, we start by selecting a warm and deep earthy tone as the fill style for the canvas. This choice adds richness and depth to the backdrop, setting the stage for our emoji grid to come alive.

Using the canvas context method fillRect(), we cover the entire canvas with this chosen color, effectively creating a solid-colored background that serves as the canvas upon which our emoji grid will be displayed.

This step lays the foundational element for our project, providing a pleasing background against which our emojis will be showcased.

Grid Iteration

To systematically position emojis across our canvas, we employ a nested loop structure, enabling us to traverse both the rows and columns of the grid. This approach allows for precise placement of emojis at regular intervals, ensuring uniform coverage and efficient use of available space.

Firstly, we calculate the number of columns and rows needed to cover the entire width and height of the canvas. This calculation ensures comprehensive coverage across the canvas, accommodating emojis without overcrowding or leaving empty spaces. Within the nested loop structure, we iterate through each row and column, determining the position of each emoji based on its respective row and column index. Through this iterative process, emojis are systematically positioned at regular intervals across the canvas, creating a grid layout.

By carefully orchestrating this grid iteration process, we achieve a balanced distribution of emojis, optimizing their placement for visual appeal and spatial efficiency. This methodical approach ensures that our emojis are seamlessly integrated into the canvas, enhancing the overall aesthetic and user experience.

Emoji Placement

In our endeavour to precisely position emojis within each grid cell, we calculate the coordinates of the emoji's center point. This calculation is crucial as it considers the size of the cells and ensures that the emojis are appropriately positioned within their designated spaces. Adjustments to the starting position are made iteratively to accommodate the grid layout seamlessly.

During each iteration, we create a new instance of an Emoji object at the calculated coordinates. Before rendering it onto the canvas, we configure the emoji with the necessary size parameter to ensure consistency and visual coherence across the grid. Subsequently, we invoke the draw() method associated with each emoji object, effectively rendering it onto the canvas at its designated position. Through this meticulous process of emoji placement, we craft visually compelling grids with precise design and spacing.

This attention to detail captivates viewers and ignites their imagination, inviting them to explore and discover the intricacies of our carefully curated composition. Each grid cell serves as a canvas for a unique emoji, enriching the viewing experience and encouraging interaction with our thoughtfully crafted creation.

Introduction to Animation Loop

In the realm of web animation, time acts as the canvas upon which creators weave intricate tapestries of movement and expression. At the core of this creative process lies the animateLoop function—a masterful symphony of timing and coordination that infuses our visual creations with vitality.

Central to our exploration is the animation loop, a fundamental concept in dynamic web animation. It embodies a continuous cycle of rendering and updating, serving as the backbone of our endeavour.

Through the mastery of JavaScript, we harmonize the passage of time with the rendering of visual elements. This results in a seamless and immersive experience that captivates the senses and sparks the imagination.

```
function animateLoop(timestamp) {
    const now = performance.now();
    const elapsed = now - lastRender;

    if (elapsed > fpsInterval) {
        lastRender = now - (elapsed % fpsInterval);

        tick++;
        drawEmojiGrid();
    }

    animationID = requestAnimationFrame(animateLoop);
}
```

The animateLoop function serves as the beating heart of our animation, orchestrating the passage of time and coordinating the rendering of visual elements with precision and finesse.

Time Measurement

To ensure precise timing and synchronization within our animation loop, we initiate the process by capturing the current timestamp using the performance.now() method. This action marks the exact moment when the animation loop begins execution, providing a reference point for measuring time intervals.

Subsequently, during each iteration of the animation loop, we calculate the elapsed time since the last render cycle. This calculation enables us to understand the temporal dynamics of our animation by quantifying the duration between successive frames.

By analysing these time intervals, we gain valuable insights into the rate at which our animation progresses, facilitating the implementation of precise timing mechanisms and synchronization strategies.

This foundational step sets the stage for orchestrating smooth and coherent animations, ensuring a seamless viewing experience for our audience.

Frame Rate Control

Within our animation loop, we exert control over the frame rate by introducing a parameter called fpsInterval. This parameter acts as a threshold against which we compare the elapsed time since the last frame was rendered.

By monitoring this comparison, we guarantee that rendering occurs at a consistent and controlled pace, thus regulating the speed at which frames are displayed. This deliberate constraint prevents the animation from executing too rapidly, which could potentially lead to performance issues and detract from the overall user experience.

Maintaining a controlled frame rate enhances the fluidity of motion within our animation, ensuring smooth transitions between frames and a more immersive viewing experience for our audience.

By imposing these constraints, we strike a balance between visual appeal and optimal performance, ultimately enhancing the quality and reliability of our animation.

Rendering Invocation

Within our animation loop, we introduce a crucial parameter known as fpsInterval. This parameter serves as a benchmark against which we measure the elapsed time since the last frame was rendered.

By comparing this elapsed time against the fpsInterval, we exert precise control over the frame rate. This meticulous monitoring ensures that rendering occurs at a consistent and controlled pace. By regulating the speed at which frames are displayed, we prevent the animation from running too swiftly, which could potentially strain system resources and diminish the user experience.

Maintaining a controlled frame rate is paramount for enhancing the fluidity of motion within our animation. Smooth transitions between frames contribute to a more immersive viewing experience for our audience, allowing them to engage with our content seamlessly.

By imposing these constraints, we strike a delicate balance between visual appeal and optimal performance. This approach ultimately elevates the quality and reliability of our animation, ensuring that it captivates viewers while delivering a seamless and enjoyable experience.

Introduction to Performance Optimization

Now, we focus on performance optimization, a crucial task aimed at maximizing the efficiency and responsiveness of our web animations.

By strategically using JavaScript, we seek to unlock the full potential of our creations, enhancing their smoothness and energy while minimizing computational load and resource use.

This effort ensures our animations run fluidly and dynamically, providing an engaging experience without unnecessary strain on system resources.

```
let lastRender = 0;
const fps = 60;
const fpsInterval = 1000 / fps;
let animationID;
```

Harnessing Frame Rate Control

Controlling the frame rate of our animations is a cornerstone of performance optimization. This strategic approach involves setting limitations on how often frames are rendered, which allows us to finely balance visual quality with computational efficiency.

The goal is to maintain smooth and responsive animations across various devices and viewing conditions. By regulating the frame rate, we optimize the performance of our animations, ensuring they run smoothly without overburdening the device's resources. This control is particularly crucial for maintaining a consistent user experience across different platforms and screen sizes.

By harnessing frame rate control, we prioritize both visual and computational efficiency, creating animations that are not only visually appealing but also responsive and enjoyable to interact with.

This attention to detail ultimately enhances the overall user experience and ensures our animations perform optimally across a diverse range of environments.

Frame Rate Definition

At the start of our animation process, we establish the desired frame rate by defining a constant called "fps". This constant represents the target number of frames we aim to render per second.

Setting this frame rate serves as a baseline for assessing the rendering performance of our animation and guides our optimization strategies.

By specifying a target frame rate, we have a clear benchmark to gauge the responsiveness and smoothness of our animation. This allows us to identify any discrepancies between the actual frame rate achieved during rendering and our desired target. Such insights are invaluable for fine-tuning our animation to meet performance goals and enhance the overall user experience.

The frame rate, defined by the fps constant, provides a standardized metric for evaluating rendering performance and serves as a reference point for optimization
within our animation project.

Frame Rate Interval Calculation

To ensure precise control over the frame rate of our animation, we calculate the interval between consecutive frames using a variable called fpsInterval. This interval represents the optimal duration between each frame render, allowing us to synchronize animation updates seamlessly.

To compute the fpsInterval, we start by determining the target frame rate, which is typically expressed in frames per second (fps). Then, we calculate the duration of one frame by dividing one second (which equals 1000 milliseconds) by the target frame rate. This computation yields the ideal time interval between each frame render, ensuring that our animation progresses at the desired pace.

By synchronizing animation updates with the passage of time through this calculated interval, we maintain a consistent and controlled frame rate, resulting in smooth and fluid animations. This meticulous approach to frame rate interval calculation facilitates optimal performance and enhances the overall quality of our animation.

Enhancing Animation Loop Efficiency

Efficiency serves as the cornerstone of performance optimization, particularly within the animation loop, a pivotal element in dynamic web animations. In this crucial component, we prioritize meticulous timing and resource management to minimize computational overhead and maximize rendering efficiency. By meticulously orchestrating timing mechanisms, we ensure that animation updates occur at precisely the right moments, minimizing unnecessary computations and resource consumption.

This precise control over timing enables us to synchronize animation actions seamlessly, resulting in fluid and cohesive motion. Furthermore, we strive to optimize resource utilization within the animation loop.

By managing the allocation and release of resources such as memory and processing power, we minimize wastage and maximize efficiency. This proactive approach helps to mitigate performance bottlenecks and ensures that our animations run smoothly across a variety of devices and platforms.

Ultimately, by enhancing the efficiency of our animation loop, we deliver a seamless and immersive user experience. Through careful management of timing and resource utilization, we create dynamic web animations that captivate and engage users while maintaining optimal performance and responsiveness.

Initialization of lastRender

By initializing lastRender to zero, we establish a starting point from which we can accurately track the passage of time within our animation loop. This precise timekeeping mechanism enables us to control and synchronize the timing of our animation updates with precision.

Throughout the animation loop, we continuously update the value of lastRender to reflect the current timestamp, allowing us to calculate the elapsed time between frames dynamically. This information is instrumental in maintaining consistent frame rates and ensuring smooth and fluid animations.

The initialization of lastRender is a foundational step in our animation process, enabling us to achieve precise timing control and synchronization, ultimately enhancing the quality and performance of our animations.

Animation ID Management

In the pursuit of dynamic control over the animation loop, we incorporate a variable known as animationID. This variable serves as a unique identifier for the callback function provided to the requestAnimationFrame() method.

When you call requestAnimationFrame(), the browser returns an animationID that uniquely identifies the instance of the animation loop. By storing this animationID, you gain the ability to gracefully terminate and resume the animation loop as required. This management of the animationID empowers you to optimize resource utilization effectively.

For instance, if the animation is paused or no longer needed, you can use the cancelAnimationFrame() function, passing the stored animationID as an argument, to halt the animation loop and conserve system resources. When the animation needs to be resumed, you can simply initiate a new animation loop, leveraging the stored animationID to seamlessly continue where you left off.

By implementing this approach, you not only enhance overall performance but also ensure a smoother and more efficient animation experience for users. When the animation is paused or no longer required, you can stop the animation loop, freeing up system resources and preventing unnecessary computations. This can lead to improved performance, especially on devices with limited resources.

Furthermore, when you resume the animation, the stored animationID allows you to pick up where the animation left off, providing a seamless and uninterrupted experience for the user. This can be particularly beneficial in scenarios where the user needs to pause the animation, such as when switching to a different tab or when the application loses focus.

In conclusion, the use of the animationID variable in the animation loop is a powerful technique that enables you to effectively manage and control the animation process. By leveraging this approach, you can optimize resource utilization, enhance performance, and deliver a more polished and responsive animation experience to your users.

Unleash Motion: Initiating Dynamic Animation with Flair

At the core of our journey lies the concept of animation initiation a foundational step in creating dynamic and engaging web experiences.

Through the power of JavaScript, we enable our creations to break free from the static constraints of the digital realm, embarking on a transformative journey that captivates the users and sparks the imagination.

```
function startAnimation() {
    animationID = requestAnimationFrame(animateLoop);
}
```

The startAnimation function serves as the initiator of the animation loop, the engine that sets in motion a cascade of visual transformations.

When this function is invoked, it triggers a series of events that breathe life into our creations, orchestrating a symphony of movement and expression that captivates and delights the viewer.

Requesting Animation Frame

At the core of the startAnimation function lies the invocation of requestAnimationFrame, a vital browser API that plays a pivotal role in orchestrating the animation sequence. This function schedules the execution of a callback function to occur just before the next repaint cycle of the browser window.

By passing the animateLoop function as the callback parameter to requestAnimationFrame, we establish a recursive loop mechanism.

With each invocation of requestAnimationFrame, the animateLoop function is called, driving the animation forward by updating the visual state of our elements in sync with the browser's repaint cycle. This recursive loop ensures that our animation progresses smoothly, with each successive frame rendered at the optimal time determined by the browser.

By leveraging requestAnimationFrame, we synchronize our animation updates with the browser's rendering pipeline, resulting in a seamless and efficient animation experience for the user.

Animation ID Assignment

When we initiate the animation loop, we capture the unique identifier returned by the requestAnimationFrame function and assign it to the animationID variable. This identifier serves as a vital reference point for controlling the animation loop, enabling us to gracefully pause or resume the animation as needed.

By storing the animationID, we gain precise control over the animation process, allowing for dynamic management that can conserve system resources and optimize overall performance.

Invoking the startAnimation function marks the transition from static imagery to dynamic motion. This transition not only enhances the visual appeal but also invites users on an engaging journey of exploration and discovery, transcending the traditional boundaries of the digital realm.

As each animation frame is rendered, users are drawn deeper into a captivating visual experience that fosters a sense of interactivity and wonder. The fluidity of the animation creates a more immersive environment, encouraging users to interact and explore further.

The ability to control the animation loop dynamically through the animationID is a powerful feature. It ensures that the animation can adapt to varying conditions and user interactions, providing a responsive and efficient user experience.

By effectively managing the animation loop, we can optimize performance, enhance user engagement, and create a visually compelling narrative that keeps users enthralled and invested in the digital experience.

Orchestrating Animation Initialization

The window.onload event handler acts as the gateway to our animated realm, orchestrating a synchronized chorus of function calls that lay the groundwork for dynamic movement and engagement. It signals that the webpage and all its associated resources have finished loading, providing the perfect moment to initiate our animated journey.

This event handler ensures that our animations commence at precisely the right time, captivating audiences and immersing them in a world of motion and interaction.

```
window.onLoad = () => {
    adjustCanvasSize();
    initializeGUI();
    startAnimation();
};
```

Canvas Adjustment

At the onset of our process, we initiate the adjustCanvasSize function, a pivotal step aimed at dynamically resizing the canvas element to align perfectly with the dimensions of the browser viewport. This meticulous adjustment ensures that our canvas, the cornerstone of our digital environment, seamlessly adapts to the diverse array of screen sizes encountered across different devices and platforms.

The significance of this meticulous canvas resizing process cannot be overstated, as it serves as the foundation upon which we construct immersive and responsive visual experiences. Through this deliberate effort, we endeavor to engage and captivate users regardless of the device they may be using, whether it's a desktop computer, tablet, or mobile phone.

By tailoring the canvas dimensions with precision to match those of the viewport, we craft a cohesive and harmonious user experience that transcends the limitations imposed by varying screen sizes.

This commitment to responsiveness not only enhances usability but also infuses our visual content with fluidity and dynamism, thereby elevating the overall quality of interaction and engagement.

GUI Initialization

After adjusting the canvas, we move on to activating the initializeGUI function, a crucial phase in our process dedicated to setting up the graphical user interface (GUI) elements that control animation parameters. This step is vital as it enhances user interaction by offering intuitive controls to manipulate different aspects of the animation.

By utilizing dat.GUI, we empower users to customize animation settings in real-time, giving them a greater sense of control and engagement within the digital environment.

The significance of the initializeGUI function goes beyond mere configuration; it symbolizes a conscious effort to democratize the animation experience, putting control directly into the user's hands. By providing an interface for adjusting parameters like speed, direction, or visual effects, we enable individuals to tailor their experience according to their preferences and creative instincts.

Furthermore, integrating dat.GUI aligns with our overarching commitment to user-centric design principles, where accessibility and ease of use are top priorities.

By utilizing a library known for its simplicity and efficiency, we ensure that even newcomers can navigate the interface effortlessly, unlocking the full potential of our animation capabilities.

Animation Start

Now that we've carefully adjusted the canvas dimensions and set up the graphical user interface (GUI), we're ready to embark on the next phase of our journey: initiating animation. This exciting moment begins with the startAnimation function, which signals the start of a captivating visual spectacle within the digital realm.

As the startAnimation function kicks into gear, it triggers the animation loop an orchestrated series of events that bring about a cascade of visual transformations on the canvas. Each cycle of this loop injects static imagery with dynamic motion, captivating the senses and sparking the imagination of the observer. A key aspect of our animation's appeal is the seamless blending of frames, where transitions flow smoothly.

This smooth progression from one frame to the next crafts an immersive experience for the viewer, drawing them deeper into the unfolding narrative and inviting them on an explorative journey beyond the boundaries of the digital landscape.

Behind the scenes, precise function calls choreograph the movement and transformation of visual elements, guiding them through a mesmerizing dance. Static visuals evolve into dynamic spectacles that mesmerize and captivate observers, pushing the boundaries of traditional animation.

In essence, the initiation of animation marks a transformative moment in our digital creation, where static imagery comes alive with dynamic motion, blurring the lines between reality and imagination. Through the artful manipulation of visual elements and the seamless execution of animation loops, we aim to transport users on a captivating journey that inspires wonder and ignites creativity.

Orchestrating Animation Resizing

The window.onresize event handler serves as the linchpin of our animation resizing strategy, orchestrating a symphony of function invocations that synchronize animation dimensions with changes in viewport size.

```
window.onresize = () => {
    adjustCanvasSize();
    cancelAnimationFrame(animationID);
    startAnimation();
};
```

Canvas Adjustment

At the outset, we invoke the adjustCanvasSize function, a crucial step in our process aimed at dynamically resizing the canvas element to perfectly match the updated dimensions of the browser viewport. This adjustment ensures that our canvas, the fundamental visual medium of our digital landscape, seamlessly adapts to the diverse array of screen sizes encountered across different devices and platforms.

The significance of this meticulous canvas resizing process cannot be overstated, as it serves as the cornerstone upon which we build immersive and responsive visual experiences. By tailoring the canvas dimensions to precisely align with the viewport, we establish a solid foundation for captivating and delighting users, regardless of the device they may be utilizing.

The adaptability afforded by the adjustCanvasSize function is pivotal in creating a cohesive and harmonious user experience. It ensures that our visual content is presented in an optimal manner, free from distortion or cropping, regardless of the device's screen dimensions.

This commitment to responsiveness not only enhances usability but also imbues our digital creations with a sense of fluidity and dynamism, elevating the overall quality of user interaction.

Animation Termination

After adjusting the canvas, we take an essential step to ensure the stability and integrity of our animation control system: invoking the cancelAnimationFrame function. This action gracefully stops any active animation loop that might be running. Halting the animation before resizing helps prevent potential rendering issues that could arise from conflicting or inconsistent processes.

This proactive measure ensures a smooth and seamless transition during canvas adjustments, preserving the visual quality of our animation. Stopping the animation loop before resizing also enhances the stability of our system. It avoids unintended behaviors or glitches that could result from simultaneous rendering processes, making the animation experience more reliable and predictable.

In short, by calling cancelAnimationFrame after adjusting the canvas, we prioritize the stability and consistency of our animation, ensuring a smooth and visually appealing user experience.

Animation Restart

After resizing the canvas and terminating the animation, we take the essential next step: restarting the animation. This is achieved by invoking the startAnimation function, which initiates a new animation loop. By restarting the animation loop, synchronized with the updated dimensions of the canvas and viewport, we ensure seamless transitions and optimal visual fidelity.

This synchronization is crucial for maintaining the consistency of the animation, as it adapts dynamically to changes in the canvas size and viewport configuration.

With each frame rendered in the new animation loop, the visuals are adjusted to fit the resized canvas, resulting in a fluid and visually pleasing animation experience.

By restarting the animation loop in this manner, we uphold the integrity of our animation and deliver a seamless user experience that seamlessly adapts to changes in the environment. The process of restarting the animation following canvas resizing involves invoking the startAnimation function, initiating a new animation loop that is synchronized with the updated canvas dimensions.

This ensures that our animation remains visually appealing and responsive, even in the face of dynamic changes in the viewing environment.

***

Here are some challenges where you can put your learnings into practice:

1. Creating an Emoji Class

Objective: Define an Emoji class and create an instance of it

Task:

- Create a new HTML file with a <script> block.
- Define an Emoji class with properties for the emoji character and its position.
- Create an instance of the Emoji class and log it to the console. (to view the console, you can press Ctrl + Shift + I)

2. Adding a Draw Method to the Emoji Class

Objective: Add a draw() method to the Emoji class and use it to render the emoji on the canvas.

Task:

- Extend the Emoji class with a draw() method.
- Use the draw() method to render the emoji on a canvas.

3. Controlling Emoji Properties with dat.GUI

Objective: Use dat.GUI to control the properties of an Emoji instance.

Task:

- Include the dat.GUI library in your HTML file.
- Create a GUI to control the position of the emoji.

4. Responsive Canvas Resizing

Objective: Make the canvas resize dynamically to fit the window size.

Task:

- Create a new HTML file with a <canvas> element.
- Use JavaScript to make the canvas resize when the window size changes.

5: Creating an Emoji Grid

Objective: Render a grid of emojis on the canvas.

Task:

- Create a new HTML file with a <canvas> element.
- Use JavaScript to draw a grid of emojis on the canvas.

6: Creating a Basic Animation Loop

Objective: Implement a basic animation loop to move an emoji across the screen.

Task:

- Create a new HTML file with a <canvas> element.
- Use JavaScript to animate an emoji moving across the canvas.
- Optimize the animation loop to ensure smooth performance.

7: Creating a Dynamic Emoji Animation

Objective: Implement a dynamic animation that changes speed based on user input.

Task:

- Create a new HTML file with a <canvas> element.
- Use dat.GUI to allow users to control the speed of the emoji animation.

Putting it All Together: Final Showcase

Ladies and gentlemen, the moment we've all been waiting for has arrived! It's time to experience our project come to life in real-time!. Get ready to be amazed as we unveil our latest creation. I invite each and every one of you to scan the QR code and immerse yourselves in the captivating animation.

As you engage with the animation, you will have the opportunity to dynamically alter its characteristics. Feel empowered to adjust its size, speed, and position along both the x and y axis.

Chapter 6

The Art of Emoji Design: Crafting Expressive Icons

Principles of Effective Emoji Design

In today's expansive digital landscape, where words can occasionally fall short in conveying the full depth of our emotions, emojis have emerged as a universal language of expression.

Crafting these tiny symbols is an art form that delicately balances clarity, universality, and emotional resonance.

Clarity and Simplicity

At the core of every successful emoji lies the principle of clarity and simplicity. These icons are intended to be swift and clear representations of emotions and concepts, easily understood at a glance.

By stripping away unnecessary details, emojis transcend language barriers, speaking a universal visual language that resonates with people worldwide. Much like punctuation marks in our digital conversations, each symbol carries the weight of a thousand words, instantly conveying our feelings and thoughts.

To achieve clarity, designers must focus on the essential features that define each emoji. Simplified forms, bold lines, and distinct shapes contribute to the recognizability and comprehensibility of emojis.

This simplicity ensures that even at small sizes, emojis remain legible and effective in conveying their intended messages.

Consistency

Consistency is another crucial aspect of emoji design. A cohesive set of emojis maintains a harmonious style and theme, ensuring they are easily recognizable and reinforcing their meanings across various contexts. This consistency helps embed these playful icons into our collective consciousness, making them instantly familiar regardless of where or how they're used.

Maintaining a consistent design language involves using uniform line weights, color palettes, and stylistic elements throughout the emoji set. This uniformity not only aids in user recognition but also strengthens the overall visual coherence of the emojis, contributing to a seamless user experience.

Cultural Sensitivity and Universality

Designers must also consider cultural references to ensure universality in emoji design. While some symbols may be globally recognized, others might not resonate with certain segments of the diverse digital audience. The goal is to create emojis that transcend cultural boundaries, speaking to the universal language of emotion that connects us all.

To achieve this, designers should conduct thorough research and engage with diverse communities to understand various cultural perspectives.

Avoiding culturally specific symbols and opting for more universally understood imagery can help create emojis that are inclusive and relevant to a global audience.

Emotional Resonance

Emojis are fundamentally about expressing emotions. Each icon should evoke a specific feeling, whether it's joy, love, or affirmation.

From the subtle curve of a smile to the bold outline of a heart, emojis aim to create an intimate connection with users, tapping into universal human emotions that transcend linguistic differences.

Achieving emotional resonance requires careful consideration of facial expressions, body language, and symbolic elements.

Designers must ensure that the emotions conveyed are clear and relatable, enabling users to express their feelings accurately and effectively.

Versatility

The importance of versatility in emoji design cannot be overstated. A well-crafted emoji has the remarkable ability to convey a broad spectrum of emotions and ideas, enabling users to express themselves with a rich array of nuances and depth. This versatility enhances digital communication significantly, adding multiple layers of meaning and subtlety to our interactions.

Whether conveying joy, sadness, frustration, or amusement, a versatile emoji can capture the essence of complex human emotions in a simple, visual form.

This capability not only enriches the way we communicate but also fosters a deeper understanding between individuals in a digital context.

Accessibility

Moreover, accessibility plays a crucial role in emoji design. It is imperative that every emoji, no matter how intricate or straightforward, remains clear and legible to all users.

Ensuring that emojis are accessible to everyone, regardless of their abilities, is essential for promoting inclusivity in digital communication. An accessible emoji design means that individuals with visual impairments, cognitive disabilities, or other challenges can understand and use these symbols effectively.

This inclusivity ensures that digital platforms remain welcoming and usable for the widest possible audience, thereby supporting the principle that everyone should have equal opportunities to participate in digital interactions. Accessibility considerations include using high-contrast colors, providing alternative text descriptions, and ensuring that the icons are distinguishable even at smaller sizes.

The principles of clarity and simplicity, consistency, cultural sensitivity, emotional resonance, versatility, and accessibility are foundational to effective emoji design.

As digital interactions continue to evolve, the role of emojis as a universal language of expression will undoubtedly become even more significant, underscoring the importance of thoughtful and intentional design in this ever-changing landscape.

Tools and Software for Creating Custom Emojis

In today's world of modern communication, emojis have evolved from simple pictograms into a vibrant and essential part of our digital language. These tiny, expressive icons can convey emotions, reactions, and even complex ideas with just a single tap or click.

As our reliance on emojis grows, so does the demand for customization and personalization. This brings us to the exciting field of emoji design, where creators use various tools and software to craft unique and memorable icons that reflect the diversity of human expression.

Adobe Illustrator: Precision and Scalability

Adobe Illustrator stands as a leading tool in emoji creation, renowned for its precision and scalability. Illustrator provides designers with a robust set of tools for crafting emojis with crisp lines and smooth curves.

Whether it's a playful smiley face or a detailed object, Illustrator offers the flexibility and control needed to bring any emoji concept to life. The ability to create scalable vector graphics ensures that emojis remain sharp and clear at any size, making Illustrator an indispensable tool for professional designers.

Key Features:

- **Precision Drawing Tools:** Pen tool, anchor points, and Bezier curves for exact control.
- **Scalability:** Create vector graphics that maintain quality at any size.
- **Layer Management:** Organize elements efficiently for complex designs.

- **Color Control:** Extensive color libraries and gradient tools.

Adobe Photoshop: Versatility in Raster Graphics

For those who prefer working with raster graphics, Adobe Photoshop is an excellent choice. With its extensive editing capabilities and versatile brush tools, Photoshop enables designers to create emojis with rich textures, vibrant colors, and intricate details.

From subtle shading to bold strokes, Photoshop allows for unparalleled creativity in emoji design. The software's ability to handle complex image manipulations and effects makes it ideal for detailed and textured emoji creations.

Key Features:

- **Advanced Brush Engine:** Customizable brushes for varied textures and effects.
- **Layer Styles:** Apply shadows, glows, and other effects easily.
- **Color Correction:** Powerful tools for adjusting and enhancing colors.
- **Photo Manipulation:** Integrate photo elements seamlessly into designs.

Sketch: Simplicity and Power in Vector Editing

Sketch is another favorite among designers who seek a balance of power and simplicity in vector editing. Its intuitive interface and robust vector editing tools streamline the emoji design process, allowing creators to focus on their ideas without getting bogged down by complexity.

Whether crafting sleek icons for digital interfaces or whimsical characters for messaging apps, Sketch offers the flexibility and ease of use that designers appreciate.

Key Features:

- **User-Friendly Interface:** Clean and intuitive design for ease of use.
- **Powerful Vector Tools:** Comprehensive tools for precise vector manipulation.
- **Symbols and Reusable Components:** Streamline repetitive tasks with reusable elements.
- **Integration and Collaboration:** Seamless integration with other design tools and platforms.

Procreate: Versatility for Hand-Drawn Illustrations

Procreate is a versatile platform especially popular among artists and illustrators who prefer a hands-on approach to emoji creation. It provides a canvas for crafting hand-drawn or illustrative emojis with precision and flair.

Whether sketching rough concepts or adding finishing touches to a polished design, Procreate offers a wealth of tools and features tailored to the needs of emoji creators. Its robust brush engine and intuitive touch interface make it a favorite for detailed and expressive emoji designs.

Key Features:

- **Extensive Brush Library:** Wide range of brushes for different artistic styles.
- **High-Resolution Canvas:** Create detailed artworks without compromising quality.
- **Layer System:** Advance capabilities for complex designs.
- **Touch Controls:** Intuitive gestures and controls for efficient workflow.

Emoji Builder Apps

They offer a compelling alternative for those looking to streamline the creation process. These apps provide simplified interfaces and pre-made assets, making it easy for anyone to design their own emojis, regardless of their design background.

From drag-and-drop interfaces to customizable templates, emoji builder apps democratize the creation process, allowing users to express themselves with a personal touch.

Key Features:

- **Pre-Made Assets:** Libraries of ready-to-use elements.
- **Drag-and-Drop Interface:** Simplifies the design process for beginners.
- **Customization Options:** Adjust colors, shapes, and features easily.
- **Accessibility:** User-friendly for all skill levels.

Digital communication is always evolving, and so are the tools for creating custom emojis. Designers can use vector-based precision with Adobe Illustrator, unleash creativity with hand-drawn illustrations in Procreate, or explore other powerful tools like Adobe Photoshop, Sketch, and specialized emoji builder apps.

Each tool offers unique strengths to match any creative need, making it easy to craft captivating and delightful emojis.

Guidelines for Designing Emojis that Align with Branding

In the realm of digital branding, emojis have emerged as powerful symbols that infuse emotion and personality into a brand's identity. Designers tasked with integrating emojis into a brand's messaging must navigate the delicate balance between creativity and consistency, ensuring that each icon reflects the brand's essence and resonates with its audience.

Understanding the Brand's Identity

The foundation of successful emoji design begins with a deep understanding of the brand's identity. Designers must delve into the brand's visual language and ethos, gaining familiarity with its color palette, typography, and overall aesthetic.

This comprehensive grasp of the brand's visual identity is crucial for creating emojis that harmonize with existing marketing materials, promoting a sense of unity and coherence across all communication channels.

Key Considerations:

- **Color Palette:** Use the brand's established colors to ensure visual consistency.
- **Typography:** Align emoji design elements with the brand's typographic style.
- **Aesthetic:** Reflect the brand's overall look and feel in the emoji design.
- **Ethos:** Embed the brand's core values and messaging within the emojis.

Maintaining Consistency

Consistency is paramount when integrating emojis into a brand's messaging. Each icon should strictly adhere to the brand's style and tone, maintaining a uniform look that reinforces the brand's identity.

Whether the emojis are whimsical or refined, they must align with the brand's overall ethos, ensuring they appear as natural extensions of the brand rather than outliers.

Strategies for Consistency:

- **Style Guides:** Develop and adhere to an emoji style guide that outlines specific design parameters.
- **Tone Alignment:** Match the emotional tone of the emojis with the brand's messaging style.
- **Design Cohesion:** Ensure all emojis share a consistent design language, from line thickness to shading techniques.

Reflecting the Brand's Personality

Emojis must also reflect the brand's unique personality. Whether the brand is playful, professional, or a mix of both, emojis should convey this essence to the audience.

Each icon should resonate with the target demographic, evoking emotions that reinforce the brand's core values and messaging. Infusing emojis with the brand's personality helps build a deeper connection with the audience, fostering loyalty and engagement.

Techniques for Reflection:

- **Character Design:** Create emoji characters that embody the brand's traits.
- **Emotional Resonance:** Design emojis that evoke specific

emotions aligned with the brand's values.

- **Audience Insight:** Tailor emojis to the preferences and expectations of the brand's target demographic.

Offering Customization Options

Offering customization options can further enhance the brand experience, allowing users to personalize emojis while staying true to the brand's identity. By providing a platform for self-expression within the brand's visual framework, designers foster a sense of ownership and belonging among users, strengthening their affinity for the brand.

Customizable features or branded sticker packs can enrich the user experience and deepen the brand's relationship with its audience.

Implementation of Customization:

- **Editable Templates:** Provide templates that users can modify while maintaining brand elements.
- **Branded Sticker Packs:** Offer collections of stickers that users can customize with their own text or colors.
- **Interactive Features:** Integrate interactive elements that allow users to create personalized emoji variations.

By adhering to the principles of understanding the brand's identity, maintaining consistency, reflecting the brand's personality, and offering customization options, designers can create emojis that align seamlessly with the brand's identity and resonate deeply with its audience.

These well-crafted emojis forge meaningful connections that enhance brand loyalty and engagement, ensuring the brand remains vibrant and

Animating Emojis for Added Visual Appeal

When it comes to animating emojis, a delicate touch can make all the difference. The aim is to augment their meaning without overwhelming the viewer.

Subtle animations, such as a gentle sway or a nuanced change in expression, can add depth to emojis without detracting from their simplicity.

The Art of Subtle Animation

When animating emojis, a delicate touch is paramount. The goal is to enrich the emoji's meaning without overwhelming the viewer or detracting from its simplicity. Subtle animations, such as a gentle sway, a slow blink, or a nuanced change in expression, can add depth and dimension to emojis, making them more expressive and engaging.

Overly complex or exaggerated animations risk making emojis appear cartoonish or distracting, undermining their communicative purpose.

Techniques for Subtle Animation

1. **Gentle Movements:** Small, rhythmic movements can bring an emoji to life. For example, a slight bobbing motion can make a smiling face seem more welcoming.

2. **Soft Transitions:** Smooth transitions between expressions can convey a range of emotions without being jarring. A slow transition from a neutral face to a smiling one can depict growing happiness.

3. **Minimalist Effects:** Incorporate simple effects like a soft glow or a slight tilt to emphasize certain aspects of the emoji without overcomplicating the design.

Contextual Relevance

Context plays a vital role in determining the appropriate animation style for emojis. What works well in a messaging app may not be suitable for a social media platform or a professional communication tool.

Tailoring animations to suit the platform and audience is crucial for maintaining relevance and effectiveness.

Factors to Consider

1. **Platform Specifications:** Different platforms have varied technical specifications and user interaction styles. An animation that works seamlessly on a high-resolution smartphone screen might not translate well to a desktop browser.
2. **Audience Expectations:** Understanding the target audience's preferences and expectations is essential. Animated emojis designed for a younger audience on social media can be more playful, while those intended for a corporate communication tool should remain professional and understated.
3. **Intended Message:** The animation should enhance the intended message of the emoji. For instance, a heart emoji with a gentle pulsating effect can convey warmth and affection more effectively than a static image.

Rigorous Testing for Seamless Experience

Testing animations across various platforms and devices is imperative to ensure a seamless user experience. Compatibility issues or playback inconsistencies can detract from the impact of animated emojis.

By rigorously testing across different environments, designers can identify and address any issues, ensuring that users receive a consistent experience regardless of their device or platform.

Testing Strategies:

1. **Cross-Platform Testing:** Ensure that the animated emojis perform well on all major operating systems (iOS, Android, Windows, macOS) and popular browsers.
2. **Device Variety:** Test animations on a range of devices, including smartphones, tablets, and desktops, to identify and resolve any performance issues.
3. **User Feedback**: Gather feedback from a diverse group of users to understand how the animations are perceived and to identify any potential areas for improvement.

Optimization for Performance and Efficiency

Optimization is a critical consideration when animating emojis. Animated files should be optimized for file size and performance, particularly in situations where bandwidth may be limited.

By minimizing file sizes and optimizing performance, designers can ensure that animated emojis load quickly and play smoothly, enhancing the user experience without sacrificing quality.

Optimization Techniques

1. **File Compression:** Use efficient compression algorithms to reduce the file size without significantly impacting the quality of the animation.

2. **Frame Rate Management:** Adjust the frame rate to balance smoothness and performance. A lower frame rate can reduce file size and improve performance on lower-end devices.

3. **Resource Management:** Optimize the use of resources such as memory and CPU to ensure that the animations do not slowdown the overall performance of the application or platform

These animated icons add an extra layer of visual charm to various digital platforms, making the user experience more enjoyable and engaging. As digital communication continues to evolve, the thoughtful animation of emojis will play an increasingly important role in enriching interactions and conveying emotions in a visually compelling manner.

Chapter 7

Emoji Analytics & User Engagement

Understanding Emoji Usage and Sentiment Analysis

Emojis are not just whimsical symbols that add color to our messages—they represent a potent visual language that transcends the limitations of words, allowing us to convey emotions, tone, and context in our digital communications.

For businesses aiming to build deeper connections with their audience, understanding the psychology behind emoji usage is crucial.

The Psychology of Emojis

Research indicates that emojis activate the same areas of the brain as facial expressions, tapping into our innate ability to interpret emotions. This connection to our emotional processing centers makes emojis an effective tool for evoking emotional responses in digital interactions. When used thoughtfully, emojis can mirror the nuances of face-to-face communication, making online interactions feel more personal and engaging.

Emojis and Emotional Expression

Beyond their expressive power, emojis can be analyzed to uncover deeper insights into user sentiment. A simple smiley face might signal happiness or satisfaction, while a frowning face could indicate disappointment or sadness.

Consider a social media post from a brand celebrating a milestone achievement, accompanied by a series of celebratory emojis.

These symbols not only convey the brand's excitement but also invite followers to share in the joyous moment, fostering a sense of camaraderie and connection.

Sentiment Analysis Through Emojis

By examining the frequency and context of emojis used in text-based messages, businesses can gain valuable insights into the emotional tone of their audience's communications. This sentiment analysis involves analyzing the types of emojis used, the context in which they appear, and the overall emotional landscape they create

For example, a high frequency of positive emojis such as hearts, smileys, and thumbs-up icons can indicate a satisfied and engaged customer base. Conversely, the frequent use of negative emojis like frowns, angry faces, or crying icons might signal issues or dissatisfaction that need to be addressed.

Understanding these patterns allows businesses to tailor their communication strategies to better meet the emotional needs and expectations of their audience.

Strategic Use of Emojis in Business

For businesses, the strategic use of emojis can enhance marketing efforts, customer service interactions, and overall brand communication. Emojis can humanize a brand, making it more relatable and approachable. They can also serve as a bridge in cross-cultural communications, where language barriers might exist but emotions remain universally understood.

Incorporating emojis into digital marketing campaigns can amplify messages and increase engagement. For instance, a well-placed emoji in an email subject line can boost open rates, while emojis in social media posts can increase likes, shares, and comments. Additionally, using emojis in customer service communications can help convey empathy and understanding, improving the overall customer experience.

By leveraging the psychological impact of emojis and analyzing their usage patterns, businesses can gain a deeper understanding of their audience's emotional landscape. This understanding enables the creation of more meaningful and engaging communication strategies, fostering stronger connections with customers and clients.

Understanding and strategically utilizing emojis can transform digital interactions, making them more personal, relatable, and effective. As businesses continue to navigate the digital landscape, the thoughtful integration of emojis will be key to building lasting emotional connections with their audience.

Impact of Emojis on User Engagement

Emojis play a significant role in driving user engagement across various digital platforms.

One notable example of the impact of emojis on user engagement is Domino's Pizza's innovative campaign, which allowed customers to order pizza simply by tweeting a pizza emoji. This creative use of emojis not only simplified the ordering process but also sparked excitement and generated buzz among customers.

By leveraging the widespread familiarity and popularity of emojis, Domino's Pizza was able to streamline the ordering experience and encourage customer interaction on social media platforms. This, in turn, resulted in increased brand visibility, engagement, and ultimately, sales.

In email marketing campaigns, incorporating emojis in subject lines or call-to-action buttons has been shown to significantly boost user engagement metrics such as open rates and click-through rates.

For example, a study conducted by Experian revealed that adding emojis to subject lines led to a remarkable 56% increase in unique open rates for promotional emails. This surge in open rates can be attributed to the eye-catching nature of emojis, which help subject lines stand out in crowded email inboxes and capture recipients' attention more effectively.

Moreover, emojis have the unique ability to convey emotions and personality in a way that plain text alone cannot.

By strategically incorporating emojis that resonate with their target audience, marketers can create a sense of familiarity, relatability, and even playfulness, thereby enhancing user engagement and fostering a stronger connection with recipients.

A/B Testing Emoji Variations for Optimal User Response

A/B testing is like having a super-powered magnifying glass for businesses, allowing them to carefully experiment and figure out the best ways to communicate with their audience. And in this world of experimentation, emojis have become a fascinating avenue for exploration, adding a whole new layer of emotion, context, and intention to messages. Imagine you're on an online marketplace, browsing for clothes, and the retailer wants to make sure their messages really speak to you.

So, they start a journey of A/B testing, where they try out different versions of their messages, some with emojis and some without. These little emojis act like visual cues, helping to capture the essence of different product categories and sparking a subtle yet significant emotional response. For example, just adding a dress or a shoe emoji can completely change the vibe of a message, conjuring up images of style, comfort, and individuality. The process is all about precision and careful planning.

Each variation is sent out to a group of customers, and then the retailer watches closely to see how people react. They look at things like how many people click on the message, how many actually make a purchase, and how engaged customers are with the content.

Take Airbnb, for instance. They're known for their innovative approach to hospitality and user experience. They decided to experiment with emojis in their email subject lines, running A/B tests to see how it affected user engagement and bookings. They compared subject lines with emojis to those without, trying to understand the subtle but significant impact these tiny pictures had on people's behaviour.

And you know what? The results were eye-opening. Through careful testing and analysis, Airbnb discovered the perfect subject line formats that really clicked with their audience, leading to more engagement and more bookings.

In the end, A/B testing emojis is like blending art and science, where creativity meets hard data to uncover the secrets of effective communication. It's a reminder of how even the smallest details can make a big difference in the ever-changing world of online interaction.

As businesses navigate this dynamic landscape, A/B testing becomes an invaluable tool, helping them refine their messaging, optimize their strategies, and ultimately, connect better with their audience.

Leveraging Emojis for Branding and Marketing Campaigns

In the realm of branding and marketing, the utilization of emojis has become a great strategy, infusing communications with vibrancy. Emojis, those small yet expressive icons, offer a versatile tool for companies seeking to inject personality and flair into their campaigns, thereby forging deeper connections with their target audience.

One notable example of this is Coca-Cola's innovative emoji-driven advertising campaign, which stands as a testament to the power of these digital symbols. Departing from its traditional branding approach, Coca-Cola replaced its iconic logo with a series of emojis symbolizing happiness and positivity. This bold move not only captured the attention of younger demographics but also embodied Coca-Cola's core brand message of spreading joy and optimism. By harnessing the emotive potential of emojis, Coca-Cola effectively conveyed its values and connected with consumers on a more emotional level, transcending language barriers and cultural divides.

Similarly, Taco Bell recognized emojis and leveraged them to create a unique and interactive marketing experience. Through the creation of the "Taco Bell Emoji Engine", the fast-food chain invited customers to engage with their brand in a playful and dynamic manner.

Users were encouraged to tweet emojis representing their cravings, prompting Taco Bell to respond with personalized menu suggestions tailored to their preferences. This innovative campaign not only capitalized on the popularity of emojis but also fostered deeper engagement and brand loyalty among consumers. By integrating emojis into their branding strategy, Taco Bell succeeded in humanizing their brand and forging genuine connections with their audience.

In essence, the strategic use of emojis in branding and marketing campaigns offers a compelling avenue for companies to differentiate themselves in a crowded marketplace. Emojis possess the unique ability to convey emotions, evoke nostalgia, and facilitate communication in a concise and visually engaging manner. By embracing emojis as a central component of their messaging, companies can inject personality, creativity, and authenticity into their campaigns, ultimately driving deeper engagement and fostering lasting connections with their audience.

As the digital landscape continues to evolve, the integration of emojis into branding and marketing strategies will undoubtedly remain a powerful tool for companies seeking to leave a memorable impression in the hearts and minds of consumers.

Ethical Considerations in Emoji Analytics and User Data Privacy

In today's digital world, where every online interaction leaves a trail of data, ethical considerations around emoji analytics and user data privacy are more important than ever. As businesses use emojis to gain insights into user behaviour, they must prioritize protecting user data and maintaining ethical standards.

A major concern is how social media platforms and businesses collect and use emoji data. In an era where data is often called the "new oil," the temptation to analyze emoji usage patterns is strong. However, businesses need to be transparent and accountable in their data collection practices.

Users should know how their emoji usage data is being collected, stored, and used. Privacy policies should be clear and easy to understand, allowing users to make informed decisions about their data.

Compliance with data privacy regulations like the General Data Protection Regulation (GDPR) and the California Consumer Privacy Act (CCPA) is crucial. These regulations have strict rules about how user data, including emoji usage, can be collected and processed. Businesses must get explicit consent from users before collecting their data and provide ways for users to access, correct, or delete their data.

By following these regulations and adopting privacy-focused practices, businesses can build trust with their audience. Transparency creates trust, and when users feel their privacy is respected, they are more likely to engage and share their data.

Chapter 8

Emoji Security & Privacy Considerations

In recent years, emojis have become an essential part of our digital communication landscape. These small, colorful icons allow us to infuse our messages with emotions, nuances, and expressiveness that text alone often fails to convey.

From a simple smiley face to intricate depictions of activities and objects, emojis help bridge the gap between face-to-face and digital interactions, making our conversations more vibrant and engaging.

However, the widespread use of emojis comes with unique security and privacy concerns that are frequently overlooked. While they enrich our online interactions, they also introduce potential risks that need to be carefully considered.

Understanding Emoji Encoding

Emojis, those small pictorial symbols we frequently use in our digital communications, are far more intricate than they appear at first glance. Although they seem to be simple, fun additions to our messages, emojis are actually encoded characters that can have significant implications, particularly in the realms of digital communication and security.

One of the primary functions of emojis is to inject emotions and expressions into our otherwise text-based conversations. They help make our messages more engaging and relatable by conveying feelings that words alone might struggle to express. This seemingly straightforward task, however, is complicated by the diverse array of platforms and devices we use to send and receive these messages. Each platform—be it Apple, Google, Samsung, or any other—interprets and displays emojis in its own unique way, giving rise to what we can refer to as the "emoji encoding dilemma".

To illustrate, consider the scenario where you send a smiley face emoji from your iPhone to a friend who uses an Android phone. The smiley face that you perceive as a friendly gesture might be rendered differently on their device, potentially leading to miscommunication. This variation in emoji interpretation might seem trivial in casual conversations but can have more serious consequences in other contexts. Malicious actors, for instance, might exploit these differences by crafting messages that appear innocuous on one platform but can trigger harmful actions on another.

This inconsistency poses a significant challenge not only for the user experience but also for security. Cybercriminals can leverage these discrepancies to send messages that seem safe on one device but could execute harmful code on another.

Consequently, emojis could become a potential vector for security breaches, adding a layer of risk to their seemingly benign nature.

Beyond security concerns, the complexity of emoji encoding also complicates data processing and analysis. In fields like text mining or sentiment analysis, the same emoji might be interpreted differently depending on the platform, which can affect the accuracy and reliability of the analysis.

For example, an emoji that conveys happiness on one platform might be interpreted as conveying sarcasm or indifference on another, leading to skewed data and misleading results.

Addressing these challenges requires a multifaceted approach.

Firstly, there is a need to standardize emoji rendering across different platforms to minimize misinterpretation and ensure a consistent user experience. The Unicode Consortium, the organization responsible for overseeing emoji standards, plays a crucial role in this effort. They work towards creating a universal standard for emoji representation, which helps mitigate some of the inconsistencie.

Secondly, developers must implement robust security measures at the application level to handle emojis securely. This involves ensuring that their applications can process and display emojis consistently, regardless of the platform, and safeguarding against potential exploits that could leverage emoji discrepancies.

By taking these steps, developers can help protect users from security threats associated with emoji usage.

Security Implications of Emoji-Based Attacks

In the digital landscape, where communication unfolds across a vast expanse of screens and devices, the humble emoji has emerged as a universal language. These colorful pictograms, originally intended to add emotional nuance to text-based conversations, now populate our messages, emails, and social media interactions with whimsical flair. However, amidst their seemingly innocent charm lies a sinister potential – the exploitation of emojis as tools for cyber deception.

Imagine receiving a message from an unknown sender filled with cheerful emojis—smiling faces, hearts, and thumbs-up icons. At first glance, it seems harmless, even inviting. Yet, beneath this seemingly benign facade, malicious intent might be lurking, ready to trap the unsuspecting recipient.

Emojis can be used in cyberattacks in ways that are both subtle and dangerous. These emoji-based attacks exploit the trust and familiarity we associate with these symbols, making it easier for attackers to bypass traditional security defenses. Consider a phishing email adorned with a series of friendly emojis, each carefully chosen to create a sense of legitimacy and urgency. In a world where people are constantly bombarded with messages, this tactic can be highly effective in capturing the attention of unwary users. The essence of these attacks often lies in social engineering, leveraging our natural tendency to trust and connect with others.

By incorporating emojis into their malicious messages, attackers aim to create a sense of rapport and familiarity, lowering the recipient's guard. After all, who would suspect a malicious intent behind a message filled with smiling faces and thumbs-up emojis?

Emojis also possess a unique advantage in evading traditional email filters and security measures. Unlike conventional text, emojis can bypass keyword-based detection algorithms, making them effective tools for obfuscation. This allows attackers to evade detection and reach their targets.

The impact of falling victim to an emoji-based attack can be severe, leading to financial loss, identity theft, and the compromise of sensitive data. Imagine a scenario where a user, deceived by a phishing email filled with friendly emojis, clicks on a malicious link. This simple action can unleash a cascade of malware onto their system. What started as a seemingly innocent interaction quickly escalates into a full-blown security breach, with far-reaching consequences.

To mitigate the risks posed by emoji-based attacks, both organizations and individuals need to adopt a proactive approach to cybersecurity. This means cultivating a culture of vigilance and skepticism, where every message, regardless of its appearance, is scrutinized and verified. Deploying advanced threat detection mechanisms that can identify and thwart emoji-based threats is also crucial in today's interconnected world.

Education plays a critical role in enhancing resilience against such attacks. By raising awareness about the deceptive tactics used by cybercriminals and teaching practical strategies for identifying and mitigating potential threats, users can strengthen their defenses against exploitation.

Emojis, while delightful embellishments to our digital communications, also harbor a darker side. They can be used to deceive and exploit, turning innocent messages into vehicles for cyberattacks.

By understanding the security implications of emoji-based attacks and taking proactive measures to bolster our defenses, we can navigate the digital world with greater confidence and resilience.

In a landscape where even a smiley face can conceal sinister motives, vigilance is the ultimate safeguard against cyber threats.

Privacy Concerns with Emoji Usage

Choosing an emoji to accompany a message might seem like a small decision, but it can reveal a lot about a person's feelings and thoughts. Emojis like a heart-eyed smiley to show affection or a weary face to indicate tiredness provide glimpses into our emotions. However, for companies hungry for data, these simple symbols become powerful tools for profiling and surveillance.

By examining how we use emojis across messaging platforms and social media, these entities can build detailed psychological profiles, revealing our preferences, emotions, and activities with startling accuracy.

For example, if a user frequently uses emojis associated with anxiety and stress, advertisers and data brokers can infer that this person might be more susceptible to products or services that promise to reduce stress. This allows for targeted advertising campaigns designed to exploit this vulnerability.

But it's not just about targeted ads. Law enforcement agencies are also tapping into emoji analysis to identify and monitor individuals they consider potential threats. By analyzing emoji patterns in online communications, authorities can gather insights into a person's affiliations, intentions, and even potential criminal activities. This blurs the line between harmless digital expression and invasive surveillance.

The impact on user privacy is significant, raising numerous ethical and legal issues that need urgent attention. Privacy is a fundamental right, crucial to democratic societies, yet in the digital age, every keystroke and emoji leaves a trace that can be used against us.

To tackle these concerns, we need to raise awareness about the privacy implications of emoji usage and empower users to control their digital identities. This involves pushing for greater transparency and accountability in data collection practices and implementing strong privacy safeguards to prevent exploitation.

Technological innovations, such as encryption and privacy-preserving algorithms, offer promising ways to protect user privacy in this age of pervasive data collection.

By prioritizing privacy by design and incorporating privacy-enhancing technologies into digital communication platforms, developers can help mitigate the risks posed by emoji-based profiling. This ensures that users retain control over their personal data.

Examples of Privacy Concerns:

- **Targeted Advertising:** If a person often uses emojis indicating stress, advertisers could target them with ads for stress-relief products, potentially exploiting their emotional state.

- **Surveillance by Authorities:** Law enforcement agencies could analyze emoji use to track individuals, which might lead to unwarranted surveillance based on misinterpreted digital expressions.

- **Data Brokers:** Companies that buy and sell personal data could compile detailed profiles based on emoji use, further eroding user privacy and potentially leading to identity theft or fraud.

- **Social Manipulation:** By understanding a user's emotional state through their emoji usage, malicious actors could manipulate individuals by tailoring messages or content to exploit their current feelings.

- **Message Content Analysis:** Messaging platforms could analyze emoji usage to gain insights into private conversations, using this data for targeted advertising or selling it to third parties without users' explicit consent.

Political Campaigns: Political entities could analyze emoji usage to profile voters' political leanings or emotional responses to political events, leading to targeted political advertising and potentially influencing election outcomes.

Emojis have become a fun and common way to communicate online, but they also come with serious privacy concerns. As technology and data analysis methods get more advanced, the risk of emoji data being misused increases.

This misuse can range from targeted advertising and unwarranted surveillance to social manipulation and cybersecurity threats. The privacy issues linked to emoji usage are varied and significant.

It's crucial for users to understand these risks and for policymakers and tech companies to put strong protections in place. By doing this, we can enjoy the perks of digital expression without giving up our basic right to privacy.

Emoji-based Social Engineering

In human interactions, emotions play a crucial role, influencing our decisions and behaviors in both obvious and subtle ways. Emojis have become a powerful tool for expressing these emotions quickly and effectively. However, these seemingly innocent symbols can also be used for more sinister purposes, such as social engineering.

Imagine receiving a message filled with emojis like a smiling face, a thumbs-up, or hearts, asking for help. These symbols make the message feel friendly and trustworthy. But behind it, there could be a hidden intent to manipulate your emotions and behavior. Emojis can create feelings of empathy and connection, making them ideal tools for social engineers who want to exploit our natural emotional responses.

For example, a phishing email might use urgent emojis like a flashing red exclamation mark, a frowning face, and a ticking clock to create a sense of panic. In that moment of anxiety, you might act impulsively, clicking on a harmful link or giving away sensitive information.

Emojis are incredibly versatile and can be used to subtly influence how we feel and respond. By carefully choosing and arranging emojis, attackers can craft messages that evoke specific emotions like excitement, curiosity, or trust. Even a simple smiley face at the end of a fraudulent message can make it seem more genuine and friendly, lowering your defences.

Falling victim to emoji-based social engineering can have serious consequences, including financial loss, identity theft, damage to your reputation, and psychological distress. Imagine being tricked by a message filled with friendly emojis and urgent requests from someone you think you know, leading you to share confidential information. This seemingly harmless interaction could turn into a significant breach of trust and security.

To protect yourself from the risks of emoji-based social engineering, it's essential to be skeptical and vigilant when you see messages with emojis. Always question their authenticity and motives before taking any action. Additionally, using security measures like two-factor authentication and encryption can help protect you from phishing attacks and unauthorized access.

While emojis may seem like harmless additions to our digital conversations, they have a powerful impact on our emotions and behavior. By being aware of the risks and taking proactive steps to safeguard against them, we can navigate the digital world with greater confidence and security.

Techniques of Emoji-Based Social Engineering:

1. Social Media Manipulation

On social media platforms, emojis can be used to manipulate public perception and behavior. For example, a fraudulent account might use popular emojis to join trending conversations, gaining followers and influence before deploying a scam.

2. Mimicking Social Norms

People often mirror the behavior and communication styles of those they interact with. Social engineers can exploit this tendency by mimicking the emoji usage patterns of their targets.

By doing so, they create a sense of familiarity and trust, making the target more likely to comply with requests.

3. Creating Urgency

Emojis can enhance the sense of urgency in a message. For example, a social engineer might use a combination of alarm emojis and urgent phrases to prompt immediate action. This tactic is especially effective in phishing attacks, where the goal is to get the target to click on a malicious link or provide sensitive information quickly.

Defence Strategies:

1. Contextual Analysis

Analyzing the context in which emojis are used can help identify suspicious behaviour. Unusual or out-of-place emojis in professional or formal communication may indicate a potential social engineering attempt.

2. Verification Processes

Implementing verification processes for sensitive interactions can mitigate the risk of falling victim to emoji-based social engineering.

Verifying the identity of the sender through alternative channels before responding to urgent or emotionally charged requests is essential.

3. Tone and Content Analysis

Monitoring the tone and content of messages that contain emojis can help identify social engineering attempts. Messages that suddenly switch to a casual or overly friendly tone in an otherwise formal conversation could be a red flag.

In the digital age, where communication is often nuanced and multifaceted, emojis serve as more than just embellishments—they're potential indicators of social engineering attempts. By implementing a combination of awareness, education, technology, and collaboration, organizations can fortify their defenses against emoji-based manipulation and safeguard sensitive information and assets.

Stay vigilant, stay informed, and remember, sometimes a smiley face isn't just a smiley face.

Mitigating Emoji-related Risks

- **Education and Awareness**

To protect users from the potential risks associated with emojis, it's essential to educate them about how these symbols can be manipulated for malicious purposes. Emojis can be used to disguise links, hide malicious code, or trigger emotional responses that prompt users to act unwisely.

Providing training sessions or informational materials can help users recognize suspicious emojis or patterns of emoji usage and encourage caution. Awareness efforts should emphasize the importance of verifying the sender's identity, scrutinizing messages, and avoiding clicking on suspicious links or attachments embedded within emoji-laden messages.

- **Implementing Secure Communication Channels**

Organizations must ensure the use of secure communication channels to protect messages containing emojis from interception or tampering by malicious actors.

Secure communication channels typically employ encryption protocols such as SSL/TLS to encrypt data transmitted between users, thereby safeguarding the confidentiality and integrity of messages. By encrypting messages containing emojis, organizations can prevent eavesdroppers from intercepting sensitive information or altering emoji-based communications.

Additionally, employing end-to-end encryption ensures that only intended recipients can decrypt and access the contents of emoji-laden messages, further enhancing security and privacy.

- **Emphasis on Digital Hygiene**

Promote good digital hygiene practices among users to minimize the impact of emoji-related risks. Encourage users to regularly update their messaging apps and operating systems to patch vulnerabilities that could be exploited through emoji-based attacks.

Additionally, advise users to exercise caution when downloading third-party emoji keyboards or plugins, as these may introduce security vulnerabilities.

Examples of Emoji-related Security Incidents

1. Phishing Emails with Emojis

Imagine receiving an email that appears to be from a trusted source, like your bank, with a subject line filled with reassuring emojis such as "Secure Your Account!".

The email claims there have been suspicious activity and urges you to click on a link to secure your account. The link leads to a convincing-looking but fake login page designed to steal your credentials.

The use of emojis makes the email seem friendly and legitimate, lowering your guard and increasing the chances you'll click the link.

2. Social Media Scams

On social media platforms, scammers often use emojis to make their posts more eye-catching and engaging.

For example, a scam post might include a message like, "Congratulations! You've won a $1000 gift card! Click here to claim your prize".

The inclusion of celebratory emojis makes the message seem more exciting and credible. Once you click the link, you're taken to a site that either installs malware on your device or collects personal information under the guise of verifying your identity.

3. Malicious Code Hidden in Emojis

In a more technical attack, malicious actors can embed harmful code within seemingly innocent emoji messages. For instance, a hacker might send a message containing a series of emojis that, when rendered by certain applications, exploit vulnerabilities to execute malicious code on the recipient's device.

This can lead to unauthorized access, data breaches, or the spread of malware without the user even realizing it.

While emojis add richness and context to digital communication, they also introduce security and privacy risks that must be addressed. By understanding these risks and implementing appropriate safeguards, individuals and organizations can enjoy the benefits of emojis without compromising their security or privacy. While enhancing our digital conversations, emojis also bring security and privacy concerns.

Individuals and organizations must be aware of these risks and adopt measures to safeguard against potential threats. We can navigate the emoji landscape securely and responsibly through education, awareness, and proactive security measures.

Chapter 9

Emoji Psychology: Decoding Digital Emotions

In the vast world of digital communication, emojis have become colorful, miniature ambassadors of emotion. First created in Japan in the late 1990s, these small pictograms have become essential to our daily conversations, adding nuance and expression to our written words.

But beyond their surface charm, emojis have significant psychological power, influencing how we convey and interpret emotions online.

The Language of Emojis

Emojis, those vibrant symbols sprinkled throughout our digital conversations, have evolved into a powerful and nuanced means of expression. Far from being mere decorative elements, they transcend linguistic and cultural barriers, enabling us to communicate emotions, sentiments, and intentions with remarkable clarity and efficiency.

The Multidimensionality of Emojis

Emojis add layers of meaning and context to our messages, transforming simple text into rich, expressive communication. When words fall short, emojis step in to provide the necessary clarity and depth. For example, consider the heart emoji. In a romantic context, it symbolizes deep affection and love. In a friendship, it conveys companionship and care. In a professional setting, it can express admiration for a colleague's achievements or appreciation for their support. Each context infuses the same symbol with different shades of meaning, demonstrating the versatility of emojis.

Emotional Nuance and Context

Emojis excel at conveying tone and emotional cues, bridging the gap between face-to-face conversations and digital interactions. A simple smiley face can transform a neutral statement into a friendly one, while a crying face can express empathy and support during difficult times. These visual cues are invaluable in preventing misunderstandings that often arise from the lack of non-verbal communication in text-based interactions.

By providing emotional context, emojis enhance the clarity and effectiveness of our digital dialogues.

Consider a scenario where a manager congratulates an employee on their recent success. The message "Well done on the project" can be perceived as formal and detached. However, adding a thumbs-up emoji or a clapping hands emoji infuses the message with enthusiasm and genuine appreciation.

This small addition significantly impacts how the message is received, making it more personal and engaging.

The Universality of Emojis

One of the most remarkable strengths of emojis is their universality. While words can have different meanings and nuances in various languages, emojis often evoke similar emotional responses across cultural boundaries. This universal appeal makes emojis a powerful tool for fostering cross-cultural understanding and empathy in our interconnected world

Cross-Cultural Communication

In a globalized society, effective communication across diverse cultures is paramount. Emojis play a crucial role in this regard, as their visual nature transcends linguistic barriers. A smiley face or a heart symbol can communicate warmth and positivity regardless of the recipient's native language. This universality facilitates smoother interactions and fosters a sense of shared humanity.

For instance, a Japanese businessperson communicating with an American counterpart might use emojis to convey goodwill and friendliness. Despite potential language differences, emojis ensure that the intended emotional tone is accurately conveyed.

This capability to bridge cultural gaps enhances mutual understanding and cooperation in both personal and professional settings.

Flexibility and Adaptability

The flexibility and adaptability of emojis contribute to their widespread use and effectiveness. With a vast array of symbols representing various emotions, objects, and concepts, users can select emojis that precisely match their intended message.

This adaptability allows for personalized and contextually appropriate communication.

Enhancing Digital Interactions

In the realm of digital interactions, where brevity and immediacy are often prioritized, emojis serve as efficient tools for conveying complex ideas succinctly. A single emoji can encapsulate an entire sentence's worth of meaning, streamlining communication without sacrificing depth. This efficiency is particularly valuable in fast-paced environments like social media and instant messaging, where quick and effective communication is essential.

Moreover, emojis can be combined to create nuanced expressions. For example, a sequence of a smiling face, a heart, and a thumbs-up can convey a multifaceted message of happiness, love, and approval. This combinatory power enables users to craft messages that are both concise and rich in meaning.

Professional and Creative Applications

Emojis are not confined to casual conversations; they have found their way into professional and creative contexts as well. In marketing and advertising, emojis are employed to create relatable and engaging content. Brands use emojis to connect with their audience on a personal level, humanizing their messages and fostering a sense of community. For instance, a social media campaign promoting a new product might incorporate emojis to convey excitement and anticipation. The strategic use of emojis can make the campaign more relatable and shareable, increasing its reach and impact.

Similarly, in professional communication, emojis can enhance teamwork and collaboration. A project management platform might integrate emojis to facilitate quick and effective feedback among team members. A simple thumbs-up emoji can signal approval, while a thinking face emoji can indicate the need for further discussion. These visual cues streamline communication and improve workflow efficiency.

Emojis in Emotional Expression

In today's digital age, where much of our communication occurs through text-based platforms and social media, emojis have emerged as powerful tools for enhancing emotional expression. They serve as visual cues that complement written language, providing crucial context and nuance to our textual interactions. This chapter explores the pivotal role of emojis in digital communication, examining how they bridge the gap between written language and nonverbal cues, contribute to the overall tone of conversations, and enrich our ability to express complex emotions online.

Imagine receiving a text message that reads, "I'm fine." Without any additional context, this statement may appear neutral or ambiguous, leaving the recipient to infer the sender's emotional state. However, by accompanying this message with a sad face emoji, the meaning changes entirely. The emoji instantly communicates sadness or distress, providing valuable insight into the sender's emotions and facilitating a more empathetic response. This ability of emojis to convey emotions in a succinct and universally understood manner is one of their most significant strengths in digital communication.

In face-to-face communication, we rely on nonverbal cues such as facial expressions, tone of voice, and body language to interpret the emotions of others. However, in digital communication, these cues are often absent, making it challenging to accurately gauge the emotional tone of a message. Emojis serve as visual substitutes for these nonverbal cues, allowing individuals to convey emotions such as happiness, sadness, excitement, or frustration with clarity and precision. They act as emotional punctuation marks, enriching our textual interactions and helping to bridge the gap between written language and nonverbal cues in the digital realm.

Emojis not only convey emotions but also contribute to the overall tone and atmosphere of a conversation. For example, using a combination of laughing face emojis can signal lightheartedness and humor, while a series of angry face emojis may indicate frustration or annoyance. By incorporating emojis into their messages, individuals can effectively set the mood of a conversation and establish rapport with other participants. Emojis help to create a sense of shared understanding and emotional connection, enhancing the quality of communication in digital spaces.

In addition to enhancing emotional expression, emojis also enrich digital communication by adding depth and nuance to our interactions. They serve as emotional shorthand, allowing us to express complex feelings simply and clearly. Whether it's conveying empathy, excitement, gratitude, or concern, emojis enable individuals to communicate more fully and authentically online.

By incorporating emojis into their messages, people can convey not only the content of their words but also the underlying emotions and attitudes behind them, fostering empathy, understanding, and connection in our text-based, tech-driven world.

Cultural Variations

Emojis are indeed a universal language, but their meanings and interpretations can vary significantly across different cultures. This cultural variation adds an additional layer of complexity to emoji usage, highlighting the importance of understanding cultural nuances to facilitate effective cross-cultural communication.

One prominent example of cultural variation in emoji interpretation is the thumbs-up gesture emoji. In Western cultures, particularly in North America and Europe, the thumbs-up gesture is commonly used to signal approval, agreement, or encouragement. However, in certain parts of the Middle East, such as Iran and parts of the Arab world, the thumbs-up gesture can be interpreted quite differently. In these regions, the thumbs-up is often associated with a vulgar or dismissive gesture, similar to raising the middle finger in Western cultures. Therefore, using the thumbs-up emoji in a message intended for recipients from these cultures may lead to misunderstandings or offense.

Another example is the folded hands emoji, which typically conveys gratitude or a request for blessings in Western cultures. However, in cultures with strong religious traditions, such as India or Thailand, the same emoji may carry religious connotations, symbolizing prayer, reverence, or humility. Therefore, using the folded hands emoji in contexts unrelated to gratitude or blessings may be perceived differently by individuals from these cultures. Understanding these cultural variations in emoji interpretation is crucial for effective cross-cultural communication. It requires sensitivity to the diverse meanings and associations that emojis hold in different cultural contexts. Rather than assuming universal interpretations, individuals engaging in cross-cultural communication should be mindful of cultural differences and adapt their emoji usage accordingly.

To navigate these cultural nuances, individuals can employ several strategies. First, they can research and familiarize themselves with the cultural norms and meanings associated with emojis in specific regions or communities.

Additionally, they can seek feedback from individuals familiar with the cultural context to ensure that their emoji usage is appropriate and respectful.

Finally, when in doubt, it may be better to be on the side of caution and refrain from using emojis in cross-cultural communication.

Emojis and Emotional Intelligence

In the realm of digital communication, where the absence of face-to-face interaction often leaves gaps in conveying emotions, emojis have emerged as vibrant symbols capable of bridging that emotional divide. Their colourful expressions and playful representations serve as more than just embellishments to text; they are windows into the emotional landscape of the sender, revealing layers of emotional intelligence and the ability to navigate the complex terrain of human feelings.

Research has shed light on the correlation between emoji usage and emotional intelligence, suggesting that those who frequently employ emojis in their messages tend to exhibit higher levels of emotional awareness and adeptness in managing their own emotions as well as understanding those of others. This connection highlights the profound impact that emojis can have on our digital interactions, serving as markers of emotional literacy in the virtual sphere.

When individuals select emojis to accompany their messages, they are engaging in a process that goes beyond decoration. The choice of emojis reflects a conscious effort to accurately convey one's emotional state, requiring a nuanced understanding of both personal feelings and the intended message for the recipient. In essence, it is an act of emotional self-expression and empathy, as individuals strive to communicate their emotions effectively while also considering how they will be perceived by others.

Moreover, the use of emojis fosters a sense of connection and understanding in digital interactions. By incorporating emojis that reflect emotions such as joy, sadness, or gratitude, individuals invite a reciprocal exchange of emotions from the recipient, creating a shared emotional experience despite the barriers of distance and technology. In this way, emojis serve as catalysts for empathy, strengthening bonds and fostering a sense of community in virtual spaces.

The ability to interpret and respond to emojis within the context of a conversation is also indicative of emotional intelligence. Just as individuals carefully select emojis to convey their own emotions, they must also be attached to the emotional cues embedded within the emojis used by others. This skill requires a keen sensitivity to subtle nuances and an ability to empathize with the emotional states of those they are communicating with, thereby enhancing the quality of digital interactions.

In essence, emojis are more than just colourful icons; they are vehicles for emotional expression and connection in the digital age. As our modes of communication continue to evolve, the role of emojis in enhancing emotional intelligence and fostering meaningful connections is likely to become even more pronounced.

By embracing the power of emojis to convey emotions and cultivate empathy, we can navigate the complexities of digital communication with greater understanding and authenticity.

Real-world examples illustrating the use of emojis in various contexts

Consider a text message conversation between two partners who are planning a date night. Instead of simply saying, "Looking forward to seeing you tonight", one partner sends a message adorned with a heart and a rose emoji.

These emojis convey affection and anticipation, adding a touch of romance to the exchange and reinforcing the emotional connection between the couple.

Visualize a food blogger sharing a recipe on Instagram. Followers who try the recipe and leave positive comments might include a clapping hands emoji or a face savouring delicious food emoji to express their appreciation.

These emojis not only convey enthusiasm but also encourage further engagement within the online community, fostering a sense of solidarity among followers.

Imagine a group chat among friends planning a surprise birthday party. As the plans come together, participants use a combination of party popper, birthday cake, and partying face emojis to convey excitement and anticipation.

These emojis serve as virtual confetti, heightening the festive atmosphere and amplifying the joy of the occasion.

In each of these examples, emojis enhance communication, express emotions, and strengthen connections. Their thoughtful use fosters understanding and empathy online.

Here are some challenges where you can put your learnings into practice:

1: Analyze Emoji Sentiment

Objective: Understand how different emojis convey various sentiments.

Task:

- Create a list of commonly used emojis.
- Categorize each emoji into positive, negative, or neutral sentiment.
- Display the emojis with their sentiment categories on a web page.

2: Create an Emoji Mood Tracker

Objective: Track and visualize daily moods using emojis.

Task:

- Design a simple web app where users can select an emoji to represent their daily mood.
- Store the selected emoji with the date.
- Display a calendar view showing the selected emoji for each day.

Chapter 10

Emojis Across Cultures: Trends and Global Impact

In an age where global connectivity is at an all-time high, the use of emojis has become essential, enhancing the way we interact in our increasingly digital world.

This chapter delves into the most popular emojis used worldwide, explores their meanings, and examines how they enrich our digital interactions.

The Global Language of Emojis

Originating in Japan, emojis have rapidly spread across the globe, becoming an integral part of digital communication. From social media platforms and messaging apps to emails and websites, emojis are now embedded in virtually every digital platform. This widespread adoption highlights their universal appeal and their unique ability to convey complex emotions and ideas succinctly. Language also plays a role in how emojis are used. In some languages, certain emojis are used as shorthand for words or phrases.

For example, the peach emoji is often used as a playful representation of the word "buttocks". In other cultures, it might simply be used to represent the fruit.

Most Popular Emojis Worldwide

1. **The Smiling Face with Heart-Eyes:** Universally recognized as a symbol of love, admiration, and affection, the heart-eyes emoji is a go-to for expressing strong, positive emotions. Whether it's fondness for a person, place, or thing, this emoji encapsulates feelings of deep affection and admiration.

Example in Social Media:

- **Instagram Post:** A user posts a photo of a picturesque sunset with the caption, "Evenings like these (the emoji) #SunsetLovers #NatureBeauty."
- **Twitter Reaction:** A tweet about a newly released movie might read, "Just watched the latest blockbuster! Absolutely loved it (the emoji)".

This emoji acts as a universal symbol of admiration and love, making posts more relatable and emotionally impactful. It helps convey strong positive emotions quickly and effectively, enhancing the overall engagement with the content.

2. **The Face with Tears of Joy:** Laughter is a universal language, and the face with tears of joy emoji captures this perfectly. Used to indicate that something is so funny it brings tears to one's eyes, this emoji is a staple in light-hearted and humorous conversations across the globe.

Example in Group Chats:

- **Friends Chat:** After sharing a funny meme, someone might respond, "That's hilarious! (the emoji) I can't stop laughing!"
- **Family Group:** When a family member shares an amusing anecdote, another might reply, "OMG, that's so true! (the emoji)"

This emoji captures the essence of humour and joy, making digital interactions more expressive. It bridges the gap that textual communication often leaves, ensuring that the emotional tone is conveyed accurately and enhancing social bonds.

3. **The Red Heart:** Perhaps the most iconic and versatile of emojis, the red heart represents love, friendship, and deep affection. Its simplicity and clear meaning make it a favourite for expressing heartfelt emotions in any context, whether personal or professional.

Example in Personal Messages:

- **Text to a Partner:** "Good morning! Hope you have an amazing day (the emoji)."
- **Message to a Friend:** "Thanks for always being there for me (the emoji)."

This one is a versatile symbol of love and affection. Its inclusion in messages adds a layer of emotional depth, making the communication more meaningful and heartfelt. It helps convey feelings that might otherwise be challenging to express in words alone.

4. **The Thumbs Up:** Universally understood as a symbol of approval, agreement, or encouragement, the thumbs-up emoji is invaluable in digital communication. It's often used to give a quick affirmation or show support, making it a crucial tool in both personal and professional interactions.

Example in Workplace Communication:

- **Slack Message:** A manager might respond to a completed task with, "Great job on the report, team! (the emoji)".
- **Email Response:** "I've reviewed the document, and everything looks good. (the emoji)".

It's great for universal gesture of approval and encouragement. In professional settings, it facilitates efficient communication, offering a quick yet positive acknowledgment that helps maintain a supportive and collaborative atmosphere.

5. **The Folded Hands:** Commonly interpreted as a gesture of gratitude or prayer, the folded hands emoji is frequently used to express thanks, seek blessings, or show respect. Its versatility and deep cultural resonance make it popular in many cultures and contexts.

Example in Gratitude and Requests:

- **Thank You Note:** "Thank you so much for your help with the project (the emoji)".
- **Request for Assistance:** "Could you please send me the files by end of day? Thanks (the emoji)".

It adds a dimension of respect and gratitude to digital communication. Its versatility makes it effective in various contexts, enhancing the emotional tone of the message and fostering positive interactions.

Emojis Across Cultures

While many emojis have universal meanings, their usage can vary significantly across different cultures. Understanding these variations can enhance communication and avoid potential misunderstandings.

East Asia

In East Asian cultures, emojis often reflect traditional symbols and customs, playing a crucial role in digital communication. For instance, during the cherry blossom season in Japan, a common sight on social media is posts celebrating this natural phenomenon.

A user might share a photo of cherry blossoms with the caption, "Enjoying the beautiful Sakura blooms (the emoji)". The Cherry Blossom emoji connects the digital post to a significant cultural event, enhancing the seasonal ambiance and evoking the beauty and transience of cherry blossoms, which hold deep cultural significance in Japan.

Another culturally significant emoji is the Bowing Person emoji, particularly relevant in expressing apologies or gratitude. For example, after missing a meeting, one might text, "I'm very sorry for the inconvenience caused (the emoji)". This emoji visually represents the act of bowing, a gesture deeply rooted in Japanese culture as a sign of respect, apology, or thanks. Including this emoji in messages adds a layer of cultural sensitivity, making the apology feel more sincere and respectful.

Additionally, the Red Envelope emoji is commonly used in Chinese culture, especially during Lunar New Year celebrations. It symbolizes the tradition of giving red envelopes filled with money as a gesture of good luck and prosperity.

For example, someone might send a message saying, "Happy Lunar New Year! Wishing you prosperity and good fortune (the emoji)".

Western Countries

In Western countries, emojis are predominantly used to convey emotions and reactions in a lively and engaging manner. One of the most popular emojis is the Face with Sunglasses. This emoji is typically used to express a sense of coolness or confidence.

For instance, when someone posts a picture of themselves in a new outfit or achieving a milestone, the Face with Sunglasses emoji is often included in comments to highlight their stylishness or commendable achievement.

Seasonal emojis are also a significant part of Western digital communication, especially during holidays. For example, the Christmas Tree emoji becomes ubiquitous as the festive season approaches. It is used in messages to share holiday cheer, decorate virtual messages, or even indicate holiday-related plans. Similarly, the Jack-o'-lantern emoji is widely used during Halloween to convey the spooky and playful spirit of the season. These emojis help to visually enhance messages and bring a sense of celebration and festivity to digital interactions.

Additionally, Christmas holds deep religious significance for many, and emojis play a role in sharing this profound aspect. The Baby emoji is often used to symbolize the birth of Jesus Christ, reflecting the nativity story and the spiritual essence of Christmas. The Star emoji, representing the Star of Bethlehem that guided the Wise Men, conveys themes of guidance and hope. The Angel emoji is used to symbolize the angelic announcement of Jesus's birth to the shepherds.

These religious emojis add a deeper layer of meaning to holiday greetings, reminding everyone of the holy and joyous event that Christians celebrate.

Middle East

In the Middle East, emojis serve a vital role in expressing cultural, religious, and familial values. Emojis such as the Mosque and the Crescent Moon are commonly used, especially during significant religious periods like Ramadan. The Mosque emoji is often included in messages to indicate visits to the mosque or participation in religious activities. For instance, during Ramadan, someone might share a message saying, "Heading to the mosque for Taraweeh prayers (the emoji)", emphasizing their engagement in religious practices

Meanwhile, the Crescent Moon emoji is frequently seen in communications around Ramadan and Eid, symbolizing the lunar calendar's importance in Islamic culture. This emoji is often used to mark the beginning of Ramadan or to wish someone a blessed Eid, such as, "Ramadan Mubarak! (the emoji) May this holy month bring you peace and blessings".

Hospitality and family are also central themes in Middle Eastern digital communication. Emojis like the Family emoji are often used to emphasize family gatherings and the importance of family connections. For example, someone might post, "Looking forward to our family reunion this weekend! (the emoji)", highlighting the significance of family bonds and togetherness. These emojis not only add a personal touch to messages but also help convey deep cultural values and traditions.

Additionally, the Hot Beverage emoji is frequently used to represent the cultural importance of hospitality, often accompanying invitations for coffee or tea, such as, "Come over for a cup of Arabic coffee (the emoji)"

Latin America

In Latin American countries such as Brazil and Mexico, there is a strong cultural emphasis on expressing emotions openly and vividly. This cultural characteristic is reflected in the frequent use of heart and love-related emojis in digital communication. These emojis serve as a tool for conveying a wide range of affectionate emotions in a straightforward and impactful way.

Marketing Brands in Latin America leverage these love-related emojis to create a strong emotional connection with their audience. For example, a brand might use the red heart emoji in a promotional post to express gratitude to its customers, such as "Thank you for your support (the emoji)". Similarly, the heart eyes emoji might be used to highlight customer favourites or popular products, such as "Our new collection is here (the emoji)".

Africa

In many African countries, there is a growing trend towards using nature and animal emojis. This trend highlights the continent's rich biodiversity and the cultural significance of wildlife and nature.

The lion emoji is emblematic of strength, courage, and pride. In African cultures, the lion is often regarded as the king of the jungle, symbolizing power and leadership. This emoji is frequently used in social media posts and messages to convey these attributes. For instance, someone might use the lion emoji to describe a personal achievement or to celebrate a notable figure who embodies these qualities.

The elephant emoji is another popular choice, symbolizing wisdom, longevity, and memory. Elephants hold a revered place in many African traditions and folklore, often associated with intelligence and familial bonds. This emoji is commonly used in contexts where these themes are relevant, such as educational posts, family discussions, or environmental conservation messages.

Various plant emojis, like the tree and seedling, are used to represent growth, life, and the importance of nature conservation. These emojis are frequently seen in posts promoting environmental awareness, celebrating natural beauty, or discussing agricultural activities. They help convey a connection to the land and an appreciation for the natural environment.

The use of these emojis also extends to raising awareness about environmental issues. Social media campaigns and personal posts might include animal and plant emojis to highlight topics such as wildlife preservation, climate change, and sustainable practices. By incorporating these symbols, users can effectively communicate their advocacy for protecting Africa's natural heritage.

Australia and New Zealand

In Australia and New Zealand, there is a strong cultural emphasis on outdoor activities and adventure. This love for nature and the outdoors is reflected in the frequent use of outdoor and adventure-related emojis in digital communication. These emojis help users share their experiences and passions for outdoor activities, making their messages more vibrant and engaging.

The surfer emoji is commonly used to represent the popular activity of surfing, which is a significant part of the coastal lifestyle in both Australia and New Zealand. People often use this emoji in posts about their surfing adventures or to express their love for the sport. For example, a post might read "Catching waves (the emoji)" or "Another perfect day at the beach (the emoji)".

The swimmer emoji symbolizes the widespread enjoyment of swimming, whether in the ocean, lakes, or pools. This emoji is frequently used in messages related to swimming activities, such as "Morning swim (the emoji)" or "Cooling off in the pool (the emoji)", where it adds a visual element that highlights the activity.

Animal emojis like the koala and kangaroo are also popular, representing the unique wildlife native to these regions. These emojis often appear in social media posts to highlight encounters with these animals or to express national pride. For instance, a post might include "Spotted a koala today (the emoji)" or "Feeling proud to be Aussie (the emoji)", where these emojis help convey a connection to the local fauna and national identity.

These outdoor and adventure-related emojis help users share their love for nature and adventure sports, creating a sense of community among like-minded individuals.

They also enhance digital communication by adding a vibrant and engaging element that reflects the natural beauty and adventurous spirit of Australia and New Zealand.

While emojis are predominantly used in casual conversations, their role in professional settings is evolving. When used appropriately, emojis can enhance workplace communication by adding a human touch, expressing appreciation, and building rapport.

Guidelines for Using Emojis Professionally:

- **Know Your Audience:** Consider the preferences and cultural background of your colleagues or clients. Some may appreciate the use of emojis, while others might find them unprofessional.
- **Use Sparingly:** Emojis should complement your message, not dominate it. A well-placed emoji can enhance your point, but overuse can undermine your professionalism.
- **Context Matters:** Ensure the emoji aligns with the tone and intent of your message. A smiley face can soften constructive feedback, while a clapping hands emoji can succinctly acknowledge a job well done.
- **Avoid Controversial Emojis:** Stay clear of emojis that may be interpreted as controversial or potentially offensive.vb

Bonus Content

Emoji Riddle Challenge: Can you Decode the Symbols

Welcome to the bonus content! In this exciting adventure, we're going to delve into the world of creating a captivating emoji game. Get ready for a journey where we'll explore the art of coding, all while utilizing beginner-friendly tools like Next.js, ShacdCN UI, and Tailwind CSS to craft an interactive experience like no other.

Even if you're new to NextJS, TailwindCSS or ShacdCN UI, fear not! This project is designed for beginners, ensuring that you can follow along and create your very own emoji game with professionalism and precision, all without encountering any pesky errors. So, let's dive in and embark on this exhilarating journey together!

Setting Up Your Environment

Now, I'll guide you through the process of setting up a Next.js application with TypeScript, Tailwind CSS, and ESLint using the npx create-next-app command. This configuration establishes a robust framework for developing contemporary web applications, prioritizing efficiency, type safety, and code quality.

Before we begin, make sure you have Node.js and npm installed on your machine. If you haven't already done so, you can easily download them from the official Node.js website.

Step 1: Creating a Next.js App:

First, open your terminal and run the following command:

```
npx create-next-app@latest my-app --typescript --tailwind --eslint
```

Let's break down what each option in this command does:

- **create-next-app@latest:** This is the command to create a new Next.js application. @latest ensures that you're using the latest version of create-next-app.
- **my-app:** This is the name of your application. Replace my-app with your preferred name.
- **--typescript**: This option tells create-next-app to set up the project with TypeScript support.
- **--tailwind:** This option includes Tailwind CSS in the project setup. Tailwind CSS is a utility-first CSS framework for quickly building custom designs.

- **--eslint:** This option adds ESLint for code linting and quality assurance.

The npx command is a package runner tool that comes with npm. It allows you to execute packages without having to install them globally.

When you run the command, it will prompt you with some options. These options are typically presented to customize the setup of the app.

```
✓ Would you like to use the `src/` directory? ... No / Yes
✓ Would you like to use App Router? (recommended) ... No / Yes
✓ Would you like to customize the default import alias (@/*)? ... No / Yes
```

No for the src directory

This option typically asks whether you want to include a 'src' directory in your project structure. The 'src' directory is a common convention in many JavaScript projects, where source code files are organized.

By choosing 'No' for this option, you're indicating that you prefer to have your source files directly within the project's root directory, rather than within a separate 'src' directory. This choice can be influenced by personal preference or stick to project conventions established by your team or organization.

Yes for the App Router

Next.js offers built-in routing capabilities to navigate between different pages in your application. Selecting 'Yes' for this option indicates that you want to include the default Next.js router in your project. The Next.js router simplifies the process of defining and navigating between pages, making it easier to create multi-page applications.

No for the import alias

This option pertains to setting up import aliases, which allow you to reference files or directories using custom names or paths. Choosing 'No' for this option means you prefer not to configure import aliases during the project setup. Import aliases can improve code readability and maintainability, but they may not be necessary for every project or developer preference.

Once the setup process is complete, you can navigate to your project directory by opening your file explorer and locating the folder where you initialized your Next.js project. Once you've found it, simply double-click on the folder to open it. Alternatively, you can use the command line interface to change directories (cd) into your project folder. Here's how you can do it:

- Open your preferred command line interface (such as Command Prompt on Windows or Terminal on macOS/Linux).
- Navigate to the directory where your Next.js project is located. You can do this by using the cd command followed by the path to your project directory. For example:

```
cd path/to/your/project
```

If your Next.js project is located within a folder, you'll need to navigate to that specific folder to access the project. Here's how you can do it:

```
cd my-next-app
```

If the folder is located in a different directory, you'll need to provide the full path to that directory. For instance:

```
cd Projects
cd my-next-app
code .
```

Once you've successfully navigated to your project directory, you're ready to start working on your Next.js project! You can now open your favourite code editor to begin writing code, modifying files, and building your application.

When you navigate into your Next.js project directory, you'll encounter several files and folders that are integral to the struture and functionality of your project.

To delve deeper into our project's architecture and organization, I encourage you all to visit the official Next.js website. There, you'll find comprehensive insights into our project structure, empowering you with the knowledge to navigate and contribute effectively.

Installing ShadCN UI

ShadCN is a modern UI library designed to streamline the development of web interfaces by offering a comprehensive suite of pre-designed components and styles. Whether you're building a simple landing page or a complex web application, ShadCN equips you with the tools necessary to create polished and responsive interfaces with minimal effort.

Before we can start using the ShadCN UI library, we need to install it. For installation, you can check the official docs.

NOTE:

When setting up your ShadCN UI library, you'll be asked a series of questions to customize your setup. Here's what they mean:

- **Style:** This refers to the overall look and feel of your UI. The Default style is a good starting point for most projects. There's also New York style which has its unique components, animations, icons, and more. Compared to the Default style, the New York style has smaller buttons and cards with shadows. It also uses Radix Icons.
- **Base color:** This is the primary color used throughout your UI. In this case, Slate has been chosen. There are five options for the base color: Slate, Gray, Neutral, Zinc & stone. Each color provides a different aesthetic and feel to your user interface.
- **CSS variables for colors:** If you choose yes, colors in your UI will be defined using CSS variables. This makes it easier to change colors later on if needed.

For our project, we have opted to the New York style aesthetic, characterized by its sleek and sophisticated design elements. Key components integral to our design include a button, a dropdown menu, and an input field.

Upon the successful installation of ShacdCN and the components as mentioned earlier, our folder structure is expected to mirror the following layout:

Initiating the Project Journey

Now that all the preliminary groundwork has been completed, it's time to elevate our project even further by integrating a sleek dark mode feature. This addition will not only enhance the visual appeal of our page but also elevate the user experience to new heights. To seamlessly integrate dark mode into our project, just refer to the ShadcnUI page. From there, you can easily install the specific package tailored for implementing this feature.

After installing the package, the next step involves creating a theme provider and wrapping it within our main layout. This strategic move ensures that our dark mode feature is seamlessly integrated into the core structure of our project. By implementing a theme provider, we guarantee consistent application of the dark mode across all components, ensuring a cohesive and visually appealing user interface.

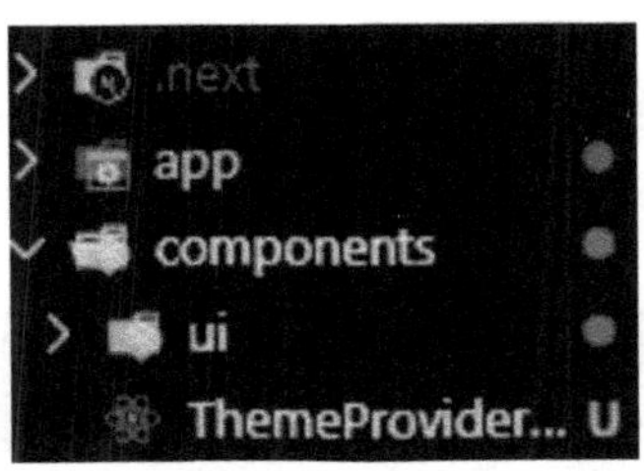

Within our components, we will establish the theme provider to seamlessly integrate dark mode. By incorporating this provider directly into our components, we ensure precise control over the application of themes throughout our project. Subsequently, we will incorporate this provider into the main layout of our application, thereby guaranteeing a consistent and engaging user experience across all levels. Following the establishment of the theme provider, our next step involves creating a dedicated file within the component's directory named "ModeToggle". This component will serve as the mechanism for toggling between light and dark modes seamlessly. By implementing this feature, we empower users to personalize their viewing experience according to their preferences.

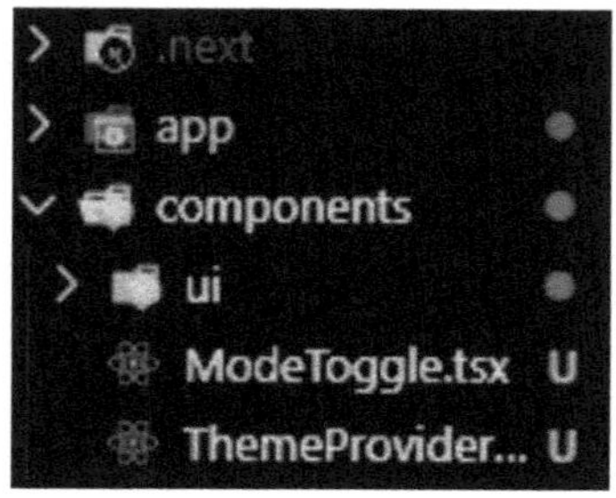

This organization keeps the components related to theming and layout separate, making it easier to manage and maintain the codebase.

To launch the application, simply execute the command npm run dev or yarn run dev in your terminal. This command will initiate the development server, allowing the application to be accessed locally at localhost:3000. By running this command, you'll be able to preview and interact with the application in real-time as you continue to develop and refine its features.

Now, we'll create a components folder within the app directory, and inside it, we'll create a file named GuessTheEmoji.tsx. This TypeScript file will serve as the primary component where we'll implement all the main functions of our project.

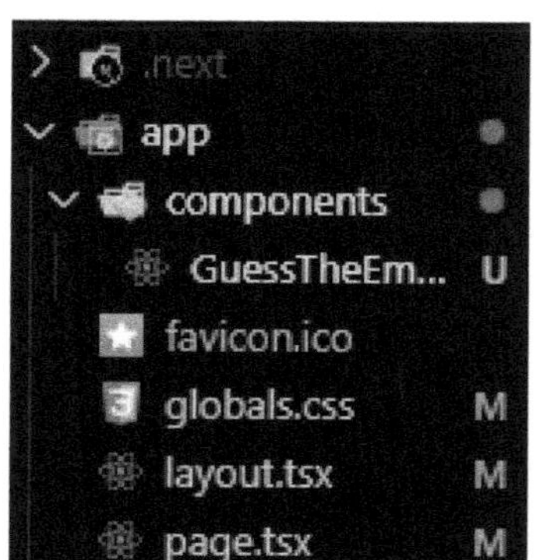

In GuessTheEmoji.tsx, we're gonna implement the core functionalities of the project, such as rendering the game interface, managing user interactions, handling game logic, and any other relevant features. Inside GuessTheEmoji.tsx, we're gonna run rafec &

it'll create a boilerplate code for react. If you don't have the "ES7+ React/Redux/React-Native" extension installed in your VS Code editor, you can install it from the Extensions tab by searching for "ES7+ React/Redux/React-Native snippets" and then clicking on the "Install" button.

```
import React from 'react'

const GuessTheEmoji = () => {
  return (
    <div>GuessTheEmoji</div>
  )
}

export default GuessTheEmoji
```

After completing the initial file setup, we will navigate to the 'page.tsx' file located within the 'app' folder. We will proceed by clearing its contents and inserting a new component. Prior to adding the component, we will create two <div> elements.

```
import { ModeToggle } from "@/components/ModeToggle";
import GuessTheEmoji from "./components/GuessTheEmoji";

export default function Home() {
  return (
    <div className="relative">
      <div className="flex justify-center items-center h-screen">
        <GuessTheEmoji />
      </div>

      <div className="absolute top-0 right-0 mt-4 mr-4">
        <ModeToggle />
      </div>
    </div>
  );
}
```

The first <div> will be assigned a className of 'relative', while the second <div> will possess a className of 'flex justify-center items-center h-screen'. Within this second <div>, we will incorporate the 'GuessTheEmoji' component. It's attributed with the relative class, denoting its positioning context within its parent container. The relative class ensures that its position remains relative to its original placement in the DOM flow.

Subsequently, the second <div> is configured with the following classNames: flex justify-center items-center h-screen. This combination of classNames is instrumental in establishing a layout structure.

- **flex:** Employs Flexbox, a CSS layout model, to render flexible containers for arranging items within it.

- **justify-center:** Positions the contained items horizontally at the center within the flex container.

- **items-center:** Vertically aligns the contained items at the center within the flex container.

- **h-screen:** Sets the height of the container to occupy the entire viewport height, ensuring a full-screen display regardless of the device's screen dimensions.

Furthermore, for the ModeToggle division, the 'absolute' attribute is specified, enabling precise positioning relative to its closest ancestor with positioning. 'top-0' is employed to align the element precisely with the top edge of its container, while 'right-0' ensures alignment with the far-right edge of the container. Additionally, 'mt-4' introduces a margin of four units at the top of the element, while 'mr-4' applies a similar margin to its right side.

After implementing these adjustments, your webpage should resemble the following design:

Now, we're gonna, start the development of our game by transitioning the entire component to utilize client functionality, alongside importing key React hooks such as useState, useEffect, useCallback, as well as components like Button and Input which we installed from ShadCN UI.

```
"use client"

import { useState, useEffect, useCallback } from "react";
import { Button } from "@/components/ui/button";
import { Input } from "@/components/ui/input";
```

Transitioning to Use Client Functionality

It involves integrating features within our game component that leverage the capabilities and resources available on the user's browser or device. In web development, the term "client" typically refers to the user's browser or device.

By utilizing client functionality, we tap into the processing power, storage, and other resources available on the user's device. This allows us to enhance the game experience by offloading certain tasks or computations to the client side, reducing server load and improving responsiveness. For example, we might implement client-side caching to store frequently accessed data locally, reducing the need for repeated server requests. We could also utilize client-side scripting languages like JavaScript to handle interactive elements, dynamic content updates, and user input validation in real-time.

Overall, transitioning to use client functionality ensures that our game interacts efficiently with the user's browser or device, optimizing performance and enhancing the overall user experience.

Importing React Hooks

React hooks are functions that enable developers to use state and other React features in functional components. Among the most commonly used hooks are:

- **useState:** This hook allows us to add state variables to functional components. State variables enable us to manage and update component data dynamically. By calling useState, we can initialize a state variable and obtain a function to update its value. This is particularly useful for managing form inputs, toggles, and other interactive elements within a component.

- **useEffect:** This hook enables us to perform side effects in functional components. Side effects may include fetching data from an API, subscribing to events, or manually changing the DOM. The useEffect hook takes a function as its argument, which will be executed after the component renders. We can also specify dependencies to control when the effect should re-run, optimizing the performance and behavior of our component.

- **useCallback:** This hook is used to memoize functions, which can help optimize performance by preventing unnecessary re-renders of child components. When we pass a callback function to a child component, useCallback ensures that the function reference remains the same across re-renders, unless its dependencies change.

This is especially useful in complex applications where performance is critical, as it minimizes the overhead of creating new functions on each render.

Importing Button and Input Components

These are standard user interface components that we'll be using in our game. Once the transition to client functionality and the importation of necessary React hooks and components are completed, our next step involves creating an array of emojis, which will play a central role in our application. Now, we're gonna start by defining our array of emojis. Each emoji will be represented as an object with two properties: emoji and name. The emoji property will hold the actual emoji character, while the name property will describe what the emoji represents.

```
const emojis = [
  { emoji: "😎", name: "smiling face with sunglasses" },
  { emoji: "🤯", name: "exploding head" },
];
```

Feel free to add as many emojis as you like to make the game more exciting!. Now that we have our array set up, we're gonna some states which will be important for our game.

```
const [currentEmojiIndex, setCurrentEmojiIndex] = useState(
  Math.floor(Math.random() * emojis.length)
);

const [guess, setGuess] = useState("");
const [isButtonDisabled, setIsButtonDisabled] = useState(true);
```

We'll start by creating a state variable named currentEmojiIndex. The useState returns an array with two elements: the current state value (currentEmojiIndex) and a function to update it (setCurrentEmojiIndex). The initial value of currentEmojiIndex is set to a random index within the range of the emojis array. Math.random() generates a random number between 0 and 1. Multiplying it by emojis.length ensures that the result is within the length of the emojis array. Math.floor() rounds down to the nearest integer, ensuring that we get a valid index.

Then, we're gonna create another state variable named guess with an initial value of an empty string "". Similar to the previous line, it returns an array with guess as the current state value and setGuess as the function to update it. This state will hold the user's input for their guess in the game. Our last state variable isButtonDisabled is declared with an initial value of true. Again, it returns an array with isButtonDisabled as the current state value and setIsButtonDisabled as the function to update it. This state controls whether a button in the game interface should be disabled or not. By setting it to true, we ensure the button is initially disabled.

In summary, we are setting up three state variables for a React component: currentEmojiIndex to manage the current emoji being displayed, guess to hold the user's input, and isButtonDisabled to control the state of a button in the game interface. These states are initialized with appropriate initial values and functions to update them, facilitating state management within the React componets.

Now, inside our return statement, we're gonna create a <div> element which is, characterized by various CSS classes assigned to it.

These classes, like "container" and "text-center", are responsible for styling the container, ensuring its content is centered horizontally within the viewport and providing padding for aesthetic spacing.

Nested within this container is an <h1> heading element, marked with classes dictating its appearance notably, a larger font size, bold text, and some margin at the bottom for visual separation. The textual content of this heading, "Guess The Emoji", serves as a clear and inviting prompt, likely signaling the start of a game.

```
return (
    <div className="container text-center mx-auto p-4">
      <h1 className="text-3xl font-bold mb-4">Guess The Emoji</h1>
    </div>
  );
```

Now, our page should look something like this:

Now, let's proceed with the implementation of the Button and Input component. We'll start by setting up a container with flexbox properties, arranging its children in a vertical column at the center of the container. It also includes a margin-bottom for spacing.

Then, we're gonna create another div with the id "emoji-display" which will serve as a placeholder for displaying an emoji. It's styled with large font size (text-5xl) and has a margin bottom for spacing.

Inside this div, another container is set up with flexbox properties, this time arranging its children in a vertical column at the center.

Then we're gonna add the input component which represents a text input field where the user can enter their guess. It receives various props such as type, id, placeholder, value, and className for styling. The value of the input field is bound to the guess state.

```
return (
    <div className="container text-center mx-auto p-4">
      <h1 className="text-3xl font-bold mb-4">Guess The Emoji</h1>
      <div className="flex flex-col items-center mb-6">
        <div id="emoji-display" className="text-5xl mb-4" />
        <div className="flex flex-col items-center">
          <Input
            type="text"
            id="guess-input"
            placeholder="Enter your guess"
            value={guess}
            className="w-full mb-4 px-4 py-2 text-xl border-2 border-gray-300 text-black dark:text-white rounded-md outline-none"
          />

          <Button
            id="check-btn"
            disabled={isButtonDisabled}
            className={`w-full ${
              isButtonDisabled
                ? "bg-gray-400 cursor-not-allowed"
                : "bg-yellow-300 hover:bg-yellow-500 text-white font-semibold rounded-md cursor-pointer"
            }`}
          >
            Check
          </Button>
        </div>
      </div>
    </div>
  );
```

Similarly, this Button component represents a button labeled "Check" that the user can interact with to submit their guess. It receives props such as id, disabled, and className for styling. The disabled state of the button is determined by the isButtonDisabled state. The button's appearance and behavior are dynamically styled based on whether it's disabled or not.

So now our page should look something like this:

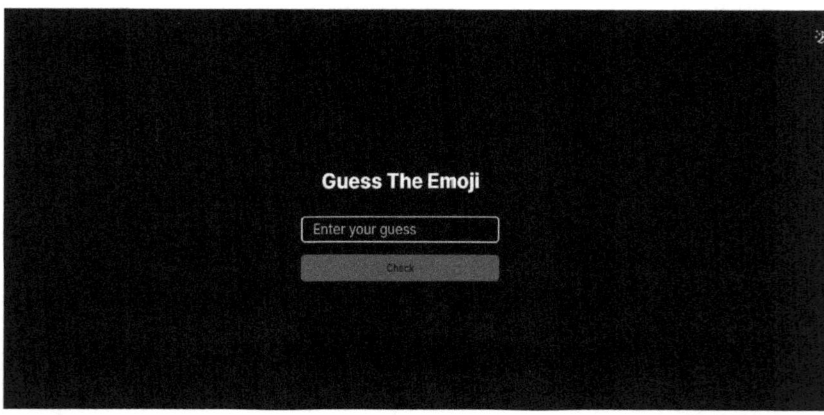

In this phase, we're refining our app's core functionalities to bring our game to fruition. We're crafting intuitive and immersive features, guided by user feedback and ergonomic design principles, to ensure a seamless and enjoyable user experience. Our goal is to create an interface that guides users through the game's various aspects, fostering engagement and delight.

We're gonna start by creating a function called displayRandomEmoji using the useCallback hook. The purpose of this function is to display a random emoji on the page.

Inside the function, we first try to find an HTML element with the id "emoji-display" using document.getElementById("emoji-display"). If such an element exists, we set its text content to the emoji corresponding to the currentEmojiIndex from an array called emojis.

```
const displayRandomEmoji = useCallback(() => {
    const emojiDisplay = document.getElementById("emoji-display");

    if (emojiDisplay) {
      emojiDisplay.textContent = emojis[currentEmojiIndex].emoji;
    }
  }, [currentEmojiIndex]);

```

```
useEffect(() => {
    displayRandomEmoji();
    setIsButtonDisabled(guess.trim() === "");
  }, [currentEmojiIndex, guess, displayRandomEmoji]);
```

Next, we have a useEffect hook. This hook is used for performing side effects in function components. Here, we want to execute two tasks whenever there is a change in currentEmojiIndex, guess, or displayRandomEmoji.

First, we call the displayRandomEmoji function we defined earlier. This ensures that whenever the currentEmojiIndex changes, a new random emoji is displayed.

Then, we update the state of a variable called isButtonDisabled. This variable is set based on whether the trimmed value of guess is an empty string. This disables a button if the guess is empty, and enables it otherwise.

In summary, this code sets up a function to display random emojis and ensures it is called whenever certain variables change. Additionally, it updates the state of a button based on the user's input.

```
const checkGuess = () => {
    const currentEmoji = emojis[currentEmojiIndex];

    if (
      guess.trim().toLowerCase() === currentEmoji.emoji ||
      guess.trim().toLowerCase() === currentEmoji.name
    ) {
      toast.success("Correct! 🎉");
    } else {
      toast.error("Incorrect! 😞 Try again.");
    }

    setCurrentEmojiIndex(Math.floor(Math.random() * emojis.length));
    setGuess("");
  };
```

Then we'll create a function called checkGuess which is responsible for validating the user's input guess against the current emoji being displayed.

First, it retrieves the current emoji object from the emojis array using the currentEmojiIndex. Then, it compares the trimmed and lowercase version of the user's guess against both the emoji property and the name property of the current emoji object. If the guess matches either the emoji or the name, it displays a success message using the toast.success function otherwise, it displays an error message using the toast.error function.

Finally, it updates the currentEmojiIndex to a new random index within the range of the emojis array length. This effectively changes the displayed emoji to a new random one. Additionally, it resets the guess state to an empty string, clearing the input field for the user to make a new guess.

In summary, this function checks if the user's guess matches either the displayed emoji or its name, provides feedback to the user accordingly, updates the displayed emoji to a new random one, and clears the input field for the next guess.

Q. What's the toast in the code?

The toast notifications in the provided code snippet are generated using the react-hot-toast library, which is a powerful tool for incorporating notification messages into React applications. These notifications serve to provide users with feedback based on their actions within the application.

To integrate react-hot-toast into your application, you'll first need to install it. Once installed, navigate to the main app layout component. Here, ensure that react-hot-toast is imported and placed at the top of the component hierarchy, preferably above the ThemeProvider. This ensures that toast notifications can be displayed regardless of where they are triggered within the application. You can customize the position of the toast notifications by specifying the desired position when initializing the ToastProvider. I configured the notifications to appear at the bottom-center of the screen.

Once the integration of react-hot-toast is complete, the next step involves incorporating the newly created functions into the input field and the button. This ensures that the application functions as intended, providing a seamless user experience. We're gonna start by the handleInputChange function which is associated with the input field, allowing it to capture user input dynamically. The checkGuess function is linked to the button's onClick event, triggering the validation of the user's input and displaying appropriate toast notifications based on the outcome.

By incorporating these functions into the input field and button elements, the application is primed to deliver a cohesive and intuitive user experience, ensuring accurate validation of guesses and prompt feedback through toast notifications.

So now, your input & the button should look like this:

```
<div className="flex flex-col items-center">
        <Input
          type="text"
          id="guess-input"
          placeholder="Enter your guess"
          value={guess}
          onChange={handleInputChange}
          onKeyDown={handleKeyDown}
          className="w-full mb-4 px-4 py-2 text-xl border-2 border-gray-300 text-black dark:text-white rounded-md outline-none"
        />

        <Button
          id="check-btn"
          onClick={checkGuess}
          disabled={isButtonDisabled}
          className={`w-full ${
            isButtonDisabled
              ? "bg-gray-400 cursor-not-allowed"
              : "bg-yellow-300 hover:bg-yellow-500 text-white font-semibold rounded-md cursor-pointer"
          }`}
        >
          Check
        </Button>
```

***

As the final lines of code are meticulously woven together, the culmination of countless hours of dedication, a remarkable achievement is born: your game, now stands complete.
With a sense of pride and excitement coursing through your veins, you find yourself on the cusp of a new chapter in your journey.

But as the last keystroke fades into the digital ether, a question arises: what's next? How do you take this creation from the confines of your development environment and unleash it upon the world?

The answer lies in the art of hosting, in bringing your creation to life on the vast canvas of the internet.

In the upcoming chapter of your adventure, you'll delve into the intricacies of web hosting, unlocking the potential to share your game with a global audience.

Through the magic of technology, you'll transform your creation into a living, breathing entity, accessible to your audience far and wide.

Before moving on to the next chapter, here are some challenges you can practice to start exploring Next.js, Tailwind CSS and ShacdCN UI.

1: Emoji Riddle Generator

Objective: Set up a basic Next.js project with ShacdCN UI and Tailwind CSS.

Task:

- Initialize a new Next.js project.
- Integrate ShacdCN UI components for layout and styling.
- Use Tailwind CSS for custom styling and responsive design.

2: Emoji Riddle Data Management

Objective: Manage and display emoji riddle data dynamically.

Task:

- Create a JSON file with emoji riddle data.
- Fetch and parse the JSON data in your Next.js project.
- Display each riddle question and emojis dynamically on a webpage.

3: Interactive Answer Submission

Objective: Implement interactive features for submitting answers to emoji riddles.

Task:

- Add a form input field for users to enter their answers.
- Validate user input against the correct answer.
- Provide feedback to users if their answer is correct or incorrect.

4: Bonus Emoji Riddle Styling

Objective: Enhance the visual appeal of your emoji riddle challenge using Tailwind CSS.

Task:

- Implement custom styling using Tailwind CSS classes.
- Design a responsive layout.
- Add animations or transitions for user interactions.

NOTE:

To enhance the user experience in your emoji riddle challenge, consider adding toast notifications for providing instant feedback to users. You can use the react-hot-toast library or the toast notification component from ShacdCN UI.

These tools are perfect for displaying success or error messages in a sleek and non-intrusive manner.

From Code to Cloud: Deploying your Game with Vercel

Congratulations! You've built an amazing game, polished every detail, and now it's time to share it with the world. In this chapter, we'll delve into the intricate process of deploying your game to the cloud using Vercel.

Vercel provides a seamless platform for deploying web applications, offering scalability, reliability, and ease of use. Let's embark on this journey from code to cloud.

Introducing Vercel

In the ever-evolving landscape of web development, the demand for powerful frameworks and robust deployment platforms has never been higher. Next.js, a React framework, has gained immense popularity due to its flexibility, performance, and ease of use in building dynamic web applications. Paired with Vercel, a cloud platform for static sites and serverless functions, developers have a combination for deploying Next.js applications effortlessly.

Vercel, formerly known as ZEIT, is a cloud platform that specializes in deploying Jamstack applications, including Next.js projects. It provides a seamless workflow for building, deploying, and managing web applications, offering features like continuous deployment, serverless functions, and global CDN (Content Delivery Network) distribution.

Key Features of Vercel:

- **Automatic Deployments:** Vercel integrates with your version control system (e.g., GitHub, GitLab) to automatically deploy your Next.js application whenever you push changes to your repository. This eliminates manual deployment processes and ensures your latest code is always live.

- **Serverless Functions:** Vercel allows you to deploy serverless functions alongside your Next.js application, enabling you to offload backend logic to scalable serverless infrastructure. This simplifies development and reduces operational overhead, as you don't need to manage servers or infrastructure.

- **Global CDN:** Vercel leverages a global CDN to distribute your application assets to edge locations worldwide, ensuring low latency and high performance for users across the globe. This improves the loading speed of your Next.js project and enhances the overall user experience.

As you embark on the journey of deploying your project, the initial step is to navigate to the GitHub website and establish a new account(if you haven't already). Once your account is ready, proceed to create a new repository on GitHub. At this point, you have the option to make the project public or private, and you can also choose whether or not to attach a license to it.

After creating the new repository, carefully follow the instructions displayed on the screen. Next, transition to

Visual Studio Code and open the terminal within the application. Finally, execute the following series of commands:

```
git init, git add ., git commit -m "Your deployment message"
```

git init

This command initializes a new Git repository in the current directory or in the directory specified. It creates a new hidden subdirectory named .git, where Git stores all the metadata and object database for the repository.

When you run git init, Git sets up all the necessary files and directories that it needs to begin tracking changes.

git add .

This command adds all the current changes in the working directory to the staging area (also known as the index) for the next commit.

The period (.) after git add signifies that you want to add all changes in the current directory and its subdirectories. You can also specify individual files or directories to add.

git commit -m "Your deployment message"

This command records the changes staged in the index into the repository's history. It saves a snapshot of the changes along with a message describing the changes. The -m flag allows you to specify a commit message inline. It's a good practice to make the commit message descriptive and concise, summarizing the changes made in the commit.

Following these steps, proceed to copy the commands provided in the second block, denoted as "or push an existing repository from the command line". Execute these commands by pasting them into the terminal and pressing enter.

Commands from "or push an existing repository from the command line" block:

These commands are typically provided by GitHub when you create a new repository online and want to push your local repository to the remote server.

git remote add origin <remote_repository_URL>: This command sets up a new remote named "origin" and associates it with the provided URL. The remote URL usually points to your repository on a Git hosting service like GitHub or GitLab.

git branch -M main: This command renames the default branch from "master" to "main". This is often done for inclusivity and to align with more respectful terminology.

git push -u origin main: This command pushes your committed changes from your local "main" branch to the "main" branch on the remote repository (specified by "origin"). The -u flag sets up tracking so that in the future, you can simply run git push without specifying the remote and branch.

Once done, return to your GitHub account and refresh the page. Boom, your entire file directory now resides within the repository. Continuing forward, venture to Vercel(or any other preferred hosting platform), and establish an account(if you haven't already). With your account set up, import your project.

As you proceed, the platform will prompt you to configure the project, allowing you to rename it if desired, adjust output settings, and manage environment variables. Given that our project is built using Next.js and lacks environmental dependencies, we can bypass the environment variable configuration step.

With the configuration complete, deploy your application. Upon successful deployment, Vercel will furnish you with a custom domain. If you wish to modify this domain, simply navigate to the domains section where you can either alter the project name or keep the existing one.

***

As you celebrate the successful completion of the game, it's not just an achievement but a significant milestone in your journey. Now, let's explore some additional steps with careful consideration, ensuring that each refinement contributes to the polished excellence of our game.

Navigate to the main layout file, typically located at app/layout.tsx. Within this file, locate the <Metadata> section. Here, you can specify essential information such as the title and description of your application. The title serves as an identifier for your app, providing users with immediate context regarding its purpose. By defining a clear and descriptive title, you can effectively communicate the essence of your application to potential users.

A favicon, short for "favorite icon", is a small graphical representation associated with a website or web application. Adding a favicon enhances brand recognition and contributes to the overall professional appearance of your application.

To integrate a favicon into your application, follow these steps:

- **Select or Create Your Favicon:** Choose an image that effectively represents your application or brand. Alternatively, you can design a custom favicon to align with your unique identity. Ensure that the image is appropriately sized formatted for optimal display.

- **Placement in the Public Folder:** Save the chosen image in the public folder of your project directory. This directory serves as the root for publicly accessible assets within your application.

- **Insertion into the Main Layout:** Once the image is securely stored in the public folder, proceed to the main app layout file (app/layout.tsx). Within the return statement of this file, insert the following code snippet.

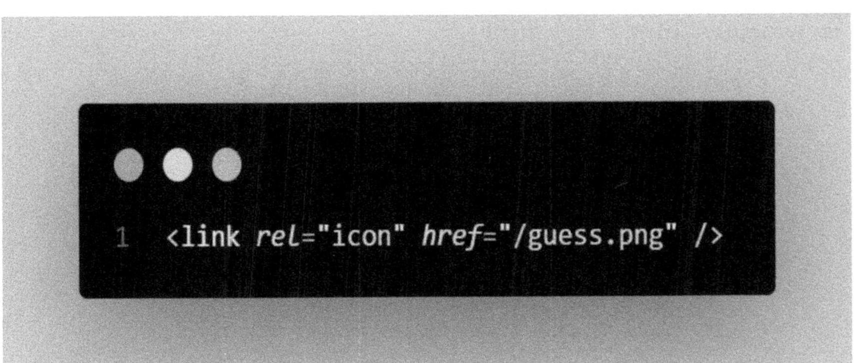

```
<link rel="icon" href="/guess.png" />
```

By incorporating this code, you establish a direct link between your application and the image, ensuring its seamless integration and display across various platforms and devices.

As we conclude our journey into the world of expressive emojis, I hope it has sparked your creativity and provided you with valuable insights for integrating playful expressions into your web design projects. You've explored the intricacies of Unicode, unlocked the potential of JavaScript animation, and embraced the art of emoji design. From understanding emoji psychology to mastering dynamic resizing and animation, you've embarked on a comprehensive exploration of this vibrant aspect of digital communication.

Reflecting on your learnings, I encourage you to experiment, innovate, and push the boundaries of what's possible with emojis in web design. Whether you're crafting captivating user experiences, conducting emoji analytics for enhanced engagement, or addressing security considerations, may this knowledge empower you to create memorable digital interactions that resonate with your audience

Your feedback is invaluable. Please share your thoughts, experiences, and insights from this journey. Your reviews will help improve future editions and contribute to our community's collective knowledge. Together, let's continue to elevate the art of web design with expressive emojis. Thank you for joining me on this adventure.

Warm regards,
StelvinSaji - Author & Editor

Let's Connect:

LinkedIn: https://www.linkedin.com/in/stelvin-saji/

GitHub: https://github.com/Stelvinsaji

Discord: chrisredfield0322

Twitter: @StelvinSaji

For further discussion and any questions you may have, please do not hesitate to reach out to me via LinkedIn or Twitter. From there, we can coordinate a suitable time for a more detailed conversation via Zoom or Twitter Spaces.

To access the source code for both the main animation and the game, simply enter the following link into your web browser: https://tinyurl.com/34bkkjt9

NOTE:

Once you've accessed the code for the game (only for the game), it's important to ensure that all necessary packages are installed. You can accomplish this by running either npm i or yarn install in your terminal.

These commands will automatically fetch and install all dependencies specified in the project's package.json file, ensuring that the game runs smoothly without any missing components.

Notes

Chapter 1: Getting Started with Emojis

1. **Asif Afzal. (2019).** "Emoji: The First Global Lan guage?". https://creativeword.uk.com/blog/language/emojis-first-global-language/

2. **Vivyan Evans. (2017).** The Emoji Code: How Smiley Faces, Love Hearts, and Thumbs Up are Changing the Way We Communicate.

3. **Ewa Puchalska. (2019).** "Why is Emoji a Vital Part of Marketing Communication?" https://napoleoncat.com/blog/marketing-emoji/

4. **Christine Van Zyl. (2023).** "Why Emojis Matter In Digital Communication?" https://www.leaguedigital.com/blogs/why-emojis-matter-in-digital-communica tion/

5. **Suzanne Scacca. (2021).** "How to Use Emojis in Web Design" https://origin-blog.mediatemple.net/de sign-creative/emojis-in-web-design-heres-what-you need-to-know/

6. **Allie Decker. (2021).** "The Ultimate Guide to Using Emojis in Email Marketing" https://blog.hubspot.com/marketing/emojia

Chapter 2: HTML Integration

1. **Stefan Gustavson. (2005).** "Simplex noise demystified"

2. **Data Arts Team. (dat.gui).** GitHub Repository https://github.com/dataarts/dat.gui

3. **Jos Dirksen. (2017). "Learning Three.js - the JavaS cript 3D library for WebGL"** https://www.packtpub.com/product/learning-threejs-the-javascript-3d-li brary-for-webgl/9781784392215

Chapter 3: CSS Styling & Page Optmization

1. **"What is a CSS Reset and Why Use One?"** https://www.cssreset.com/what-is-a-css-reset/

2. **CSS-Tricks & Reference.** Retrieved from https://css tricks.com/almanac/

Chapter 4: Interactive Emoji Magic with JavaScript

1. **Mozilla Developer Network.** https://developer.mozilla.org/en-US/docs/Web/JavaScript/Reference/Statements/const
2. **Mozilla Developer Network.** https://developer.mozilla.org/en-US/docs/Web/API/Canvas_API
3. **"JavaScript Best Practices"** https://www.w3schools.com/js/js_best_practices.asp
4. **Flafla2 (2014).** "Understanding Perlin Noise" https://adrianb.io/2014/08/09/perlinnoise.html, http://graphics.pixar.com/library/WaveletNoise/paper.pdf

Chapter 5: Animating Emojis with JavaScript: Adding Life to Web Interactions

1. **JavaScript Classes** - Mozilla Developer Network. https://developer.mozilla.org/en-US/docs/Web/JavaScript/Reference/Classes
2. **MDN Web Docs - Introducing JavaScript objects.** https://developer.mozilla.org/en-US/docs/Learn/JavaScript/Objects
3. **MDN Web Docs - CanvasRenderingContext2D.drawImage().** https://developer.mozilla.org/en-US/docs/Web/API/CanvasRenderingContext2D/drawImage

4. **Haverbeke, M. (2014).** Eloquent JavaScript: A Modern Introduction to Programming. No Starch Press.

5. Data Arts Team - dat.GUI. GitHub Repository. https://github.com/dataarts/dat.gui

6. O'Reilly Media. (2013). HTML5 Canvas.

7. MDN Web Docs - Canvas API. https://developer.mozilla.org/en-US/docs/Web/API/Canvas_API

8. W3Schools - Responsive Web Design. https://www.w3schools.com/html/html_responsive.asp

9. MDN Web Docs - Responsive Web Design Basics. https://developer.mozilla.org/en-US/docs/Learn/CSS/CSS_layout/Responsive_Design

10.Eric Rowell: HTML5 Canvas Animation Cookbook. Packt Publishing.

11. MDN Web Docs - Window.requestAnimationFrame(). https://developer.mozilla.org/en-US/docs/Web/API/window/requestAnimationFrame213

12.Best Practices for Speeding Up Your Web Sites Yahoo Developer Network. https://developer.yahoo.com/performance/rules.html

13.Grigorik, I. (2013). High Performance Browser Networking. O'Reilly Media.

14. Cody Lindely (2013). DOM Enlightenment. O'Reilly Media.

15. Mozilla Developer Network - Element.animate(). https://developer.mozilla.org/en-US/docs/Web/API/Element/animate

16. MDN Web Docs - Animation.playState. https://developer.mozilla.org/en-US/docs/Web/API/Animation/playState

17. MDN Web Docs - Element.requestFullscreen(). https://developer.mozilla.org/en-US/docs/Web/API/Element/requestFullscreen

18. MDN Web Docs - ResizeObserver. https://developer.mozilla.org/en-US/docs/Web/API/ResizeObserver

Chapter 6: The Art of Emoji Design: Crafting Expressive Icons

1. Jennifer Daniel - Talk to Me: The Evolotion of Emojs. (2020)

2. Jhonny Levanier - How to make Custom Emojis. (2021)

3. Songyang Liao - Color Affects Recognition of Emoticon Expressions. (2022)

Chapter 7: Emoji Analytics & User Engagement

1. Barbieri, F., Ballesteros, M., & Saggion, H. (2017). "Are Emojis Predictable?" https://aclanthology.org/E17-2017/

2. Connor B. (2016). "The Power of Emojis in Marketing and How to Use Them Efficiently." https://www.business2community.com/brandviews/buffer/power-emojis-marketing-use-efficiently-little-known-keyboard-shortcuts-01589862

3. Christina G. (2018). "How to Use A/B Testing to Experiment with Your Content Marketing". https://www.crazyegg.com/blog/ab-testing-content-marketing/

Chapter 8: Emoji Security & Privacy Considerations

1. Unicode Consortium - "Security Considerations". https://www.unicode.org/reports/tr36/

2. RSA Conference - The Evolving Role of Emojis in Investigations and Data Security. (2024)

3. Computerware Blog - Those Cute Little Emojis May Be Putting Your Data At Risk. (2016)

4. ManageEngine Blog - How Hackers Use Emojis to Infect Your Devices. (2023)

Chapter 9: Emoji Psychology: Decoding Digital Emotions

1. Neil C, Jan E & Joost S (2019). "The Grammar of Emoji" Constraints on communicative pictorial sequencing https://www.researchgate.net/publication/335511515_The_grammar_of_emoji_Constraints_on_communicative_pictorial_sequencing
2. Isabella B, Megan LeBlanc, Justin A & Charles A (2021). "Emojis influence emotional communication, social attributions, and information processing https://www.sciencedirect.com/science/article/abs/pii/S0747563221000443
3. Donath, J. S. (2015). "The Social Machine: Designs for Living Online". MIT Press.

Chapter 10: Emoji Accross Cultures: Trends and Global Impact

1. Unicode Consortium - https://unicode.org/emoji/charts/full-emoji-list.html
2. Laura Kerslake, Rupert W (2017) - The Semiotics of Emoji: The Rise of Visual Language in the Age of the Internet https://www.researchgate.net/publication/321976795_The_Semiotics_of_Emoji_The_Rise_of_Visual_Language_in_the_Age_of_the_Internet

3. The Future of Creativity: US Emoji Trend Report. (2022) - https://blog.adobe.com/en/publish/2022/09/13/emoji-trend-report-2022
4. Satomi Sugiyama: Kawaii meiru and Maroyaka neko. (2015) - https://firstmonday.org/ojs/index.php/fm/article/download/5826/4997
5. Daniela.D.A, Ryan.K, Eammon.O. Beyond Happy-or-Not: Using Emoji to Capture Visitors' Emotional Experience. (2020) - https://www.researchgate.net/publication/339592826_Beyond_Happy-or-Not_Using_Emoji_to_Capture_Visitors'_Emotional_Experience
6. Sharath.C.G, Ming.L, Louis.T, Lyle.H: Studying Cultural Differences in Emoji Usage across the East and the West. (2019) - https://ojs.aaai.org/index.php/ICWSM/article/view/3224

Index

1. **Marty A, Dog 'n' Bone.** "Emojis: The Secret Behind the Smile". 2015.

2. "**The Unicode Standard:** A Technical Introduction". https://www.unicode.org/standard/principles.html

3. **Domino's Pizza Emoji Ordering** - Now you can use emoji to order pizza - The Verge https://www.theverge.com/2015/5/13/8596849/use-emoji-to-order-dominos-pizza

4. **Taco Bell Emoji Engine Campaign** - Taco Bell | The Taco Emoji Engine — Dan Rosenberg (dan-rosenberg.com)

5. **Coca-Cola Emoji Advertising Campaign** - Emojis are now ad units and Coca-Cola is the first brand to use them (marketingweek.com)

6. **Airbnb A/B Testing with Emojis** - Beyond A/B Test: Speeding up Airbnb Search Ranking Experimentation through Interleaving | by Qing Zhang | The Airbnb Tech Blog | Medium

7. **Evans, V. (2017).** "The Emoji Code: The Linguistics Behind Smiley Faces and Scaredy Cats".

8. **Evans, V. (2017).** "The Emoji Code: How Smiley Faces, Love Hearts, and Thumbs Up are Changing the Way We Communicate".

9. **Laura K, & Rupert W. (2017)**. "The Semiotics of Emoji: The Rise of Visual Language in the Age of the Internet".
10. **Philip Seargeant. (2019)**. "The Emoji Revolution: How Technology is Shaping the Future of Communi cation".
11. **Lisa Lebduska. (2014).** Emoji, Emoji What for Art Thou? https://www.researchgate.net/publication/369355551_Emoji_Emoji_What_for_Art_Thou
12. **Wei Ai, Xuan Lu, Ning Wang. (2017).** Untangling Emoji Popularity through Semantic Embeddings. https://cdn.aaai.org/ojs/14903/14903-28-18422-1-2-20201228.pdf
13. **Lauren. G. (2021).** Emojis as Digital Gestures. https://www.latrobe.edu.au/news/announcements/2021/emoji-as-digital-gestures-returning-the-body-to-disembodied-communication
14. **Joon Y, N.H, S.K, J.O. (2016).** Smiley Face: Why we use emoticon stickers in mobile messanging. https://www.researchgate.net/publication/307574484_Smiley_face_why_we_use_emoticon_stickers_in_mobile_messaging
15. **Hamza. A. (2016).** Are Emojis Creating a New or Old Visual Language for New Generations? A Socio-semiotic Study. https://papers.ssrn.com/sol3/papers.cfm?abstract_id=3709343
16. **Bernardo. P, Marilia. P, David. L. (2024).** Examining the Effects of Reciprocal Emoji Use on Interpersonal and Communication Outcomes.

www.ingramcontent.com/pod-product-compliance
Ingram Content Group UK Ltd.
Pitfield, Milton Keynes, MK11 3LW, UK
UKHW021405190726
13845UKWH00028B/902

9 789334 059878